HELPING
OTHERS IN
• CRISIS •

DEALING WITH
SUICIDE

JOHN R. THROOP

David C. Cook Publishing Co.
Elgin, Illinois — Weston, Ontario

David C. Cook Publishing Co.
Elgin, Illinois—Weston, Ontario
Dealing with Suicide
© 1989 David C. Cook Publishing Co.

Published by David C. Cook Publishing Co.
850 N. Grove Ave., Elgin, IL 60120
Cable Address: DCCOOK
Designed by Christopher Patchel and Steve Smith
Photo by Paul Brackley
Illustrated by Jane Sterrett
Printed in the United States of America
Library of Congress Catalog Card Number: 88-71537

ISBN: 1-55513-010-0

CONTENTS

ACKNOWLEDGEMENTS

In writing a book on so personal a subject as suicide, I understand that I risk exposing part of myself which is painful to reveal. I also risk being misunderstood by well-meaning Christians who think that one should concentrate only on the victory that we have in Jesus Christ; a book on suicide hardly fills that bill.

So I first want to acknowledge my gratitude to Marlene LeFever, originator of this series, "Helping Others in Crisis." When I first ventured this proposal, she gave her enthusiastic endorsement—and I was off and running.

I also want to thank the people of Christ Episcopal Church in Shaker Heights, Ohio, where I was Associate Rector as I began doing research for this book. I will always be thankful for their encouragement of frank biblical sermons dealing with the tough parts of life. And I want to thank George Ross, the rector, and John McDuffie, the curate at St. Paul's Church in Akron, Ohio for preaching the same way and for providing an environment in which I could reflect on the subject matter of this book in a Christian fashion.

Along the way I have known some wonderful pastors and therapists (along with a few "clunkers," too!). But Dr. Sam Schwartz stands out as one who has been particularly helpful to me. He is a wonderful Christian layman and counselor.

My father-in-law, Roy W. Anderson, devoted some of his retirement to being something of a research assistant to me as he clipped newspaper and magazine articles on the subject of suicide. He also made helpful suggestions in the writing and presentation of the book, particularly to affirm strongly the power and presence of God.

I am grateful to my parents for their love and understanding through some very troubled years—the extent of the trouble they did not really know until I talked with them before this book was published. We all have grown.

Finally—and certainly not in order of priority—I am grateful to my wife, Isabel Anders, for her encouragement and prodding along the way to get the manuscript done in the midst of many pressing matters. And I thank her for her love for me. It was worth living, and waiting, for. So, too, my children Sarah and Emilie.

John R. Throop

INTRODUCTION

THE PHONE RANG INSISTENTLY. DREAD SWEPT OVER ME, because I was a pastor and it was the middle of the night. Fumbling for the phone, I struggled to become alert. Barely had I blurted "Hello" when an anguished voice broke in on the other end of the line.

"Pastor! This is Laurie! It's Mark. Something terrible has happened to him. He's dead!"

My heart sank like a rock. *Oh, Lord, not another one,* I groaned under my breath. "Laurie, where are you now?"

"I'm—at the hospital." She struggled to get the words out. "Can you come? Please! I need you!"

So I spent another sleepless night comforting a spouse left behind by suicide. I spent many hours in the days and weeks afterward to help Laurie put her life back together, to help her children, and to give her a sense of the grace and peace of God.

As a pastor, I've aided many families who grappled with the grief and anger that suicide brings. Sometimes they were like Laurie and her children, facing the suicide of someone in the prime of life. Other families mourned the loss of an elderly relative who believed suicide would make him or her "less of a burden." Then there were the young victims, whose dreams and goals had somehow evaporated.

Like many pastors and counselors, I have been thrown into the specialty of suicide intervention because of what I have faced in ministry. Serving in small towns, affluent suburbs, and areas of the city filled with unemployment and seeming despair, I have seen that suicide happens everywhere. It knows no boundaries of race or class. It is an ever-present—and growing— crisis.

In this book I wrestle with two difficult questions. First, why would anyone want to commit suicide? And second, what can anyone do to prevent a person from taking his or her own life?

I claim no specific psychological authority in dealing with the subject of suicide, though I have studied the subject for nearly ten years. While I have had no disciplined psychological training, I have been accountable to and have consulted with professionals in the field. Counselors, social workers, therapists, and psychologists, many of them Christians, have taught me individually. I have also attended seminars and read widely on the topic. In this book, I blend these insights from the psychological and medical fields with theological reflection born of Scripture, prayer, and the fruit of personal experience in the Christian walk.

I also know about suicide because I nearly committed it myself.

I was 13 years old at the time. My family had moved yet again, and I felt completely uprooted and severed from friendships I was beginning to make at a very important time in my life—the beginning of adolescence. We moved from a duplex home to an apartment building in a town about 15 miles away, a town where I knew no one. It was the beginning of summer vacation. What a lonely time to be a kid!

That summer I slumped into a deep depression. Perhaps part of the reason was physical, but I know it was also psychological. I spent hours in my room alone. I couldn't sleep well; I would cry for no apparent reason. All I could think about was how much I did not want to live like this. I wanted to escape to where I could be happy, to where there were friends, to where there was a future. Since none of these things seemed possible in my present life, I concluded that this life could not be worth living.

I decided that I would attempt suicide. I would jump out the window head first, falling three floors to the concrete below. A sharp ledge waited there, and I determined to hit it at just the right angle to finish me off.

One hot night I decided the time had come. I wrote a note of explanation to my family. I placed the note on the bed. I went to the window and removed the screen. Then I sat on the edge of the ledge.

But I could not jump. I cannot tell you how desperately I wanted to. I simply could not do it.

Eighteen years have passed since I tried to take my own life. I used to think that this was a deep, dark secret. If anyone knew about this "flaw" in my history, I would be judged the weaker, I felt. After all, our culture demands that we—especially men—look strong in order to be accepted. God forbid that we should show "weakness" or reveal that we are not "together" nor in control.

Yet my attempt at suicide and my journey to healing are such formative factors in my walk as a person and later as a Christian. Every suicide in which I have intervened has touched old scars long healed by God. I really know what the psalmist means when he says, "You have taken my companions and loved ones from me; the darkness is my closest friend" (Ps. 88:18). But I also know profoundly what Jesus means when He says, "I am the light of the world. Whoever follows me will never walk in darkness, but will have the light of life" (John 8:12).

I am telling something of my own story in the hope that you will know that this is not some academic piece designed only to convey information. When it comes to suicidal feelings, I have "been there." But I also mean in this book to convey statistics that will give you, the helper, an idea of the gravity of the suicide problem. Most importantly, the tools and resources in this book are meant to help you prevent or intervene in a suicide situation, and to work with a family that is trying to come to grips with the self-caused death of a loved one.

I learned some time ago the value of speaking frankly about this subject. Wanting to go beyond superficial friendships with Christian brothers and sisters, I finally ventured in a small group setting to disclose my own brush with attempted suicide. Far from being shaken by this awful revelation, two others in the group of six volunteered how their lives had been touched deeply by suicide. I shared how much Psalm 23 had come to mean to me in healing and growing. Others described how their "walk through the valley of the shadow of death" had been accompanied by the Lord in the same way.

Then, a few Sundays later, my assigned text was Psalm 23. Slowly the possibility grew in my mind. Should I use my struggle with suicide as an illustration in the sermon? It would not violate my rule against using unresolved problems as illustrations, for I had found healing some time before. Still, this was very risky. After praying over the matter for two weeks, I decided to go ahead and see what happened.

I was unafraid as I preached about the presence of God in hard times. I said as I began my story, "You know me well enough to know that this faith stuff is not worth the time of day if it does not sustain us in hard times. This 'walk through the valley of the shadow of death' is not some academic exercise to me. I have lived this verse.

9

"You see," I continued, "a few years ago, I tried to commit suicide."

As I paused, the silence was frightening.

"But obviously, I didn't succeed," I said, smiling. "For somehow, long before I was a Christian, the Lord did sustain me and, dare I say, prevented me from taking my own life. There was some glimmer of hope in there that I could not even recognize. Yet He planted it in me so that I chose to live. 'Thy rod and thy staff, they comfort me.' I am living proof of the truth of this verse. And so are you."

People were touched in many different ways that morning. But I was astonished when an elderly woman came through the line in tears, with other family members behind her. "How was it that you lived and my daughter didn't?" she cried. In her case, the sermon was especially timely. Her daughter had committed suicide just that week. The sermon provided an opportunity for further ministry to that family.

You never know what will happen when you let out "the dark secret." At the very least, you will provide hope for someone to continue living, or for a loved one to find peace and reassurance.

The subject of suicide simply must be addressed openly by the Christian community. Christian leaders must have the best material in hand to understand this frightening phenomenon of self-destructiveness, and the best tools to deal with the suicidal person or her or his family.

Properly equipped, the Christian counselor can make a real difference in favor of life for those who are distressed or on the brink of despair. Secular psychiatrists, therapists, and others can only offer part of the solution. Only the Christian can adequately address the spiritual concerns in such a situation. He or she can bring the only hope that is worth having—the loving presence of God in Jesus Christ, who has set us free from condemnation and despair.

The Good News can be literally life-saving. The Gospel offers hope to a person on the brink of suicide. It is my hope that you will find this book helpful as you make yourself available to those who consider ending their lives by their own hand. As you extend your saving hand to the suicidal person, the loving hand of God can also be felt.

May you have courage and grace to persevere as you help to save souls—and lives.

CHAPTER ONE

THE GRIM STATISTICS

THERE HAVE ALWAYS BEEN HUMAN BEINGS WHO SOUGHT TO kill themselves. From King Saul in the Old Testament to Socrates in pagan Greece, there is evidence of human self-destructiveness. Suicide is not a new phenomenon. But it is one whose rate is growing today at a frightening pace.

The American Association of Suicidology, a not-for-profit organization founded in 1968 to further the understanding and prevention of suicide, recently reported that suicide claims the lives of 30,000 Americans annually. To put it another way, 82 people commit suicide on an average day. Suicide is the eighth leading cause of death in America.

The overall rate of suicide appears to be increasing. That rate (not broken down by sex, race, or age) has increased from 10.6 deaths per 100,000 population in 1960 to 12.1 per 100,000 in 1983 (the most recent year for which statistics are available). This increase may be due to an actual rise in the number of deaths traceable to suicide, or to more accurate reporting.

Americans are not the most suicidal people in the West. The World Health Organization has concluded that residents of Denmark are the most likely to commit suicide, with a rate of 37.1 per 100,000 males and 21.2 per 100,000 females. Austrians seem to be the next most likely, with a rate of 40 per 100,000 males and 15.4 per 100,000 females.

Italians were named as the least likely suicide candidates, with a rate of 10.1 per 100,000 males and 4.6 per 100,000 females. The British were the next least likely, with a rate of 11.5 per 100,000 males and 5.9 per 100,000 females.

Statistics alone cannot suggest why Danes might be more likely than others to commit suicide, and Italians least likely. What may be learned from this survey is that suicide is not a distinctly American phenomenon, nor are Americans most likely to kill themselves.

The Person Most Likely

In America, who is the most likely suicide candidate? Many would assume male teenagers hold that position. Surprisingly, however, the most likely person to commit suicide in America is a white male over the age of 65. There are 40.2 deaths per 100,000 attributable to suicide in this category. By contrast, among white females over the age of 65, the rate is 7.2 per 100,000.

The next most likely candidate for suicide is a white male between the ages of 55 and 64, with 27.4 deaths per 100,000 population. The white male between 25 and 34 follows with 26.2 deaths per 100,000; then the white male between ages 45 and 54 (25.5); and then a white male between the ages of 35 and 44 (23.2). Only then does the white male teenager appear in the rankings—at 20.6 per 100,000.

The white male in America is by far at greatest risk for suicide. Among white women, the highest-risk age group is between 35 and 44, with a rate of 9.1 deaths per 100,000 population. Among white women in America, the suicide rate has been dropping steadily for the last 15 years.

In America's black community, suicide rates are much lower than for comparable age and sex groups among whites. The black person at greatest risk for suicide is a male between ages 25 and 34, with a rate of 19.1 deaths per 100,000. Interestingly, among black males over age 65, the suicide rate is 14.2 per 100,000, much lower than their white counterparts. The suicide rate for black women of all ages is very low. Even in the group at greatest risk—the female between ages 35 and 44—the rate is 3.5 deaths per 100,000. This peak is lower than any group of any age (except children) among white males or females or black males. (Separate statistics were not available for Hispanic or Asian Americans.)

While the statistics clearly indicate that suicides are on the rise in America, that rise is not evenly distributed. Overall, there has been a 15% increase in the last 15 years. But four groups have shown significant increases (while most other groups saw a decrease). Among black males 65 or older, a nearly 70% increase in suicide was reported. White males between ages 25 and 34 recorded a 35% increase in that period. And among white males between 15 and 24, there was a startling 50% increase. The most tragic tale the statistics tell, however, is that suicides among children, black and white, of both sexes, more than doubled in that same 15-year period. While the actual rate is still very slight compared to other age groups, for all children between ages 5 and 14 the rate per 100,000 rose from .3 to .7 between 1970 and 1985. And over the last 30 years, the rate of suicide among teenagers has nearly tripled. This rate of increase cannot be matched by any other group.

So, while the elderly white male is most likely to commit suicide when compared to all age groups, it is also true that our children and teens are at greater risk than ever before of killing themselves.

Attempted Suicides

Teenage boys have a more rapidly increasing rate of suicide than girls do, but the girls *attempt* suicide almost three times as often as the boys. More generally among teenagers, nearly half a million attempt suicide yearly, and 6,000 succeed.

This ratio between attempt and success can be seen in the wider population as well. Experts estimate that, for every completed suicide, 100 more are attempted. That would suggest that over 3,000,000 Americans in any given year will attempt suicide. Taking into account the fact that there are repeat attempts, it would be fair to estimate that almost 10% of all Americans living today have attempted suicide. It cannot be estimated how many have entertained the idea of suicide, even if they did not attempt it. The number who have *not* thought about suicide probably would be much smaller than those who have.

The ratio of attempt to completion is shocking among the elderly. For every *four* attempts, *one* succeeds.

The statistics of attempt versus completion raise a question. Do those who try really want to die? Or is the attempt rather a desperate cry for help?

One study conducted in 1976 by the American Medical Association suggests that there is considerable ambivalence in the suicidal person. The evidence from the attempters also suggests the temporary nature of the suicidal urge. The AMA study followed 886 people who had attempted suicide. Five years after their attempts, only 3.8% had actually killed themselves. Thirty-five years later, 10.9% had done so. This study did not examine whether there were repeated attempts, but other statistics suggest that another ten to twenty percent will attempt suicide again.

In four out of five cases, those who kill themselves give definite verbal or behavioral warnings before going through with the act. The suicide threat, however it is made, must be taken seriously. Attempts at suicide follow threats 70% of the time.

The How, When, and Where

What methods are used to commit suicide? In 1983 (the most recent year statistics are available) in the United States, men of all ages and races clearly preferred firearms. They were used in 64% of all reported cases. Next in order of preference was hanging or strangulation, at about 15%. Poisoning (including carbon monoxide inhalation) was preferred by 14%. Other explosives and other means were used in almost 7% of the cases.

Women also used firearms most frequently, but less than men did—at 41%. Poisoning followed at 38%, with hanging and strangulation at 11% and other explosives and other means at 10%.

As we review the statistics, we must remember that many actual suicides may go unreported—so the incidence of suicide may be a lot higher than we can tabulate. The reasons are legal, in part. Nearly all insurers will refuse to pay a death benefit when suicide is ruled the cause. There is also the sense of shame and disbelief when a loved one commits suicide, which leads to underreporting. Finally, many "accidents" are not accidents at all, but suicides carefully disguised. We would have to question whether some reported drownings were unintentional. Likewise, many experts wonder whether single-car accidents are always inadvertent. That is why insurers, for example, probe carefully into a person's background when an unaccompanied accident is the cause. It may be, therefore, that the problem of suicide is even more serious than the statistics indicate.

Many people assume that suicide is seasonal—that the rate escalates around Thanksgiving, Christmas, and New Year's, often occasions of family stress or intense loneliness. But the statistics do not bear out this assumption. Suicides occur at an equal rate throughout the year, with a slight increase in the spring. I saw this to be true in my own parish work and as a hospital chaplain. We often saw fewer cases of attempted suicide around the holidays, though family violence increased at those times.

Is there a section of the U.S. where suicide is more frequent?

If you live on the Pacific coast, you are in a population at greater risk than others in America. This may be due in part to what some observers say is a greater rootlessness and weaker family commitment in that region than in other parts of the country. If you live in the north central area, where some say roots are deeper and family ties are more binding, you are least likely to commit suicide.

Despite regional variations, suicide remains a national problem of disturbing proportions. It is a problem for the Christian church, too. After all, some of those 30,000 per year who commit suicide are Christians. Even if none were Christian, the church would still have an obligation in the name of Jesus Christ to reach out in compassion and love to those "without hope and without God in the world."

Why Do People Kill Themselves?

More often than not, the suicidal person leaves a note which gives some reason for his or her act. Other times, no note is left, no warning is issued, and no reason is given.

What are the most often cited reasons for committing suicide? What are the most frequent contributing factors, according to professionals in the mental health field?

The answers differ, of course, by age and situation. So let us survey quickly our most likely candidates, beginning with the elderly white male:

Longer Life. The white male's life expectancy has increased steadily since the early part of this century. As he lives longer, there is a greater statistical probability that he will take his own life.

Loss of Purpose. Men in American culture have been identified by their work, not by their ability to form and nurture relationships. While life expectancy has increased, retirement policies generally have not changed. The man may remain vigorous, but for legitimate or bogus reasons may have to retire at age 65—or even earlier. With retirement often comes a loss of purpose for living.

Finances. Many retirees live on a fixed income from a pension, social security, and minimal savings and investments—at most. They must live at a level significantly below that to which they had become accustomed. This adjustment is often very difficult, especially since the man does not wish to be seen as a "burden" on his family or on society.

Illness and Death. Longer life expectancy does not guarantee full health. With aging, chronic and painful illness often sets in. The man loses control of his life and often becomes deeply depressed. He must face his death. He often decides that he will go out "strong" as the "manly" thing to do. Thus he commits suicide.

This is the human side of the statistics showing the highest incidence of suicide among elderly white men. What about teenagers?

Depression. Teens undergo enormous physical, mental, and spiritual changes during adolescence. The biochemical changes frequently result in depressive states, or times of intense energy and action. Any parent of a teen can testify to wide emotional swings. It is in the deeply introspective and intense mood swings that danger may lurk, for teens look at themselves hypercritically at those times. Usually they do not have the emotional maturity or life experience to know when a problem will go away.

Broken Families. Adolescents need a support and an anchor in their rapidly changing world. Now half of all marriages end in divorce, and at least 20% of all families are headed by single parents. The support often is not there for the adolescent.

Lack of Communication. One survey suggests that teens on the average spend 14 minutes a week talking with their parents, but 25 hours a week in front of the TV. If lines of communication have not been built in the home, a tremendous emotional resource is not available to the teen when he or she needs it most. When trouble comes, the young person may feel empty or out of control and try to take the "easy" way out.

Absence of Spiritual Principles. Most teens today have not grown up with a sense of obligation to another. They do not have a knowledge of a personal God, made known in Christ, for they do not see that living God active in their parents' lives. The very thing that could give them hope and certainty when they most need it is never given to them. On the contrary, most parents stress the need to succeed, to get good grades, to go to a good college, to get into a good career. Those are ingredients for terrible stress, not for strong spiritual principles.

Drugs and Alcohol. Drugs and alcohol are widely available to teens. One study by the San Diego County Coroner's Office in 1986 examined 133 consecutive suicide cases involving those under 30 years of age. Alcohol or drugs figured in 53% of those cases. Those figures could surely be mirrored around the country.

Influence of Television and Movies. As already noted, the typical American teen watches nearly 25 hours of television each week. TV, movies, and video on cassette play an important role in shaping reality for young people (and not-so-young people as well). Television and film introduce young people to the stresses and situations of the adult world. They are not neutral media.

According to the American Academy of Pediatrics, prime-time television programs average six to eight acts of violence per hour. News programs report acts of violence and death with regularity—and often in gruesome detail.

In 1987, for example, the state treasurer of Pennsylvania called a news conference. He was under investigation for alleged wrongdoing in office. At that news conference, the man heatedly denied the allegations, then said he would not be around to take any more heat from the investigators or the press. He pulled out a handgun, waved it around, and declared that he was going to kill himself. Over the cries of reporters and his own aides, he put the end of the gun in his mouth. While the cameras quietly whirred, he pulled the trigger and blew his brains out.

The networks reported on the event, but did not run the tape. A few local affiliates used the grisly visuals, an action that was widely protested. But a barrier had been broken. Suicide had become a news item to be shown in all its graphic horror.

What about TV movies dealing with suicide? The focus of these stories (with only one exception in the last ten years), has been on the teen contemplating killing himself or herself. One study has documented that after such programs there is a discernable increase in suicide, particularly among teenagers. It appears that these programs can push a very troubled young person over the edge. In such dramas the long-term heartache of family members and friends is rarely shown; but when it is, it can generate discussion in schools and community mental health centers.

Much more work needs to be done to establish a firm correlation between TV and film depictions of suicide and a clear increase in the phenomenon. But the evidence we have thus far suggests what pastors and mental health professionals have known for some time—that these media have tremendous power to evoke emotion, and to shape perception and behavior, especially among the young.

Influence of Music. In several court cases, suicide-oriented rock lyrics and their portrayal in music videos have been alleged to lead to suicide (though so far courts have not awarded damages to survivors since a direct link could not be established).

For example, Eugene Belknap, age 18, and his friend James Vance, age 21, listened to the album *Stained Class* by the rock group Judas Priest for six hours on December 23, 1985. They were also smoking marijuana and drinking during that time. When Belknap's mother returned home, the two young men jumped out a window, taking a shotgun with them. At a nearby church playground, Belknap put the gun to his head and shot himself, dying instantly. Vance attempted the same thing, but twitched at the last moment. He blew his face apart, but lived.

The case against the rock group and the recording company is still in court at this writing. The plaintiffs' and defendants' disagreements include the question of whether the album's lyrics were suicide-oriented. In other cases, suits have been dismissed for First Amendment (freedom of expression) reasons. But in some cases the connection between lyrics and suicide seems better than circumstantial, especially when lyrics have been included in some suicide notes.

We can see the struggles which lie ahead for the prevention of suicide. Before long the "baby boom" generation will begin to reach retirement age, and some have suggested that "dying with dignity" by one's own hand will grow in popularity with this group. The number of single-parent households continues to grow, destabilizing more young people. Changing employment patterns make the teenage world even more competitive, and strong support to thrive in competition simply is not there in many homes. Unless there is renewed leadership in parenting, it is likely that teens will continue committing suicide at a rate which some call epidemic. And we may expect to see greater incidence of preteen suicide—for many younger children face stresses and pressures for which they are utterly unprepared.

What Can the Church Do?

What should be the response of the Christian community to all these statistics?

First, it is crucial that the church reaffirm its support of and ministry to families. Our society gives little or no training in how to be a parent or in how to build a family—though this situation has improved in the church during the past decade. It is vitally important that a biblical foundation be laid for Christian family life as a witness to the world of the power of the Gospel of Jesus Christ.

It is also important that churches offer qualified, biblically-rooted counseling and therapy for the troubled and for those with biochemically-related psychological problems. We have been too content to refer such people to non-Christians who are at best neutral to Christian claims and beliefs. We also have been too content only to quote Bible verses to those in crisis, telling them how they *should* live without helping them to begin living that way.

The establishment of Christian counseling and mental health centers seems an increasing trend in the churches, and one that should be welcomed. Just because a conversion takes place does not mean that sanctification has been fully realized in the believer, or that problems will go away if the person simply prays hard enough. Christian ministries which walk with people through the valley of the shadow of death need to be encouraged.

In addition to helping teenagers who may be tempted to take their own lives, we must give attention to the problems with which the elderly, particularly elderly men, contend. The fastest rate of U.S. population growth is among those age 65 and over, and, in particular, those who are 80 and older. As noted earlier, the most likely candidate for suicide is a white male age 65 or older, and for every four attempts at suicide in this group one will succeed. These facts alone should prod us to learn much more about the problems our elders face, and how the church can minister effectively to such persons. In particular, we must pay attention to the problems of the elderly black male, whose rate of death from suicide is increasing at an alarming pace.

Some churches already have raised awareness of the elderly's problems and concerns. Medical experts better understand the aging process than they used to, and researchers know more about the frequency of clinical depression in our elder population. But underneath the statistics on depression and self-inflicted death among the elderly are the intense sense of abandonment and lack of purpose among these people in our culture, and the ridicule accorded them in actual life and in media portrayal.

Christians must return to a profound understanding, grounded in Scripture, of the respect and honor to be given to our elders.

We Have the Medicine

The statistical evidence of suicide begins to show us the enormity of the problem. In addition, strong forces are at work in our culture to stress the quality of life rather than the sanctity of life as the guide for decision-making on life and death. The movement toward legalizing euthanasia will make it all the more difficult to prevent suicide, for death will be seen more and more as a "right" that a person has in decision-making rather than something society has an obligation to prevent.

While the forces promoting suicide as a way out are strong, the Christian must not lose hope. We have a responsibility to stress life as a gift God has given into our stewardship and care, and to say and show that there is no pain or temptation we are given for which we are not also given the power to endure. Then we can be valuable resources and vessels of grace to those who are hurting and troubled, who see suicide as the way out of a life without hope and meaning.

What the statistics cannot convey is the utter, naked need for God in each of these precious souls. We have the only medicine that will cure this madness, this illness! The suicidal person, perhaps more than anyone else, knows what life without God is like. He or she peers into the depths of hell. Into the midst of this pain we can bring the peace of God.

You and I are the earthen vessels. We must be willing to bring our own pain and struggle to the suicidal person, to say, "I've walked where you are." And when the person is convinced that we do know, that we have indeed walked there, we can share the real source of healing, the balm for the deep wounds. We are God's agents to turn these suicide statistics around.

May this prayer for the evening, found in the Episcopal *Book of Common Prayer*, reflect our concern for the souls behind the statistics: "Keep watch, dear Lord, with those who work, or watch, or weep this night, and give Thine angels charge over those who sleep. Give rest to the weary, bless the dying, soothe the suffering, pity the afflicted, shield the joyous; and all for Thy love's sake. Amen."

CHAPTER TWO

CASE STUDIES

W HY WOULD ANYONE WANT TO COMMIT SUICIDE? THE case studies that make up this chapter may help us to answer that question.

The Roman philosopher Seneca, actress Marilyn Monroe, rock singer Janis Joplin, writers such as Virginia Woolf and Ernest Hemingway, dictator Adolf Hitler—these are but a few of the famous people who have killed themselves. But it is the unknown suicide victims whose stories we will examine here. We will enter their worlds, trying to understand the logic, twisted as it may be, that drives people to take their own lives. We will look for common traits linking the suicidal—so that you and I can be helpful to those without hope.

Michael

What drives a teenage boy to commit suicide? The case of Michael is a composite of several teens I've known who have attempted suicide—some of whom, tragically, were successful. See whether you can discern Michael's motivations. Had you known him, at what point would you have intervened? What would you have said or done?

One pleasant April afternoon Michael walked home alone from high school in a small southwestern city. He had just finished a hard track practice, as was his routine. He was one of the strong members of the team—not the best, not often a winner, but a competitor. He was a fairly good student as well—not outstanding, but good. His marks would get him into the state university, and a track scholarship would help with his expenses. Michael had to think about these things. He was 18, ready to graduate.

Michael was good-looking—not someone who might step off the fashion pages, but clean-cut, all-American good-looking. Girls were attracted to him, and he dated several. One of the "jocks" at school, he blended in well with other sports-minded kids. He was popular in a quiet sort of way, never a leader of the pack, but a welcome participant. He and many of his friends were part of a well-attended church youth fellowship.

Michael's father, Grady, was a leader and major financial contributor at church. Working in the international division of a large construction company, Grady was absent from the family for long stretches of time. Nevertheless, he took an interest in family life. He was especially proud of his eldest son, Grady III, who would soon graduate with honors from one of the nation's top business schools. The father seemed to favor young Grady, not only because the boy was his namesake, but also because the son, like the father, was intensely competitive. Grady III had been a star athlete in college while carrying an excellent grade point average; it seemed that everything he touched turned to gold.

Walter was the next son, a hard-drinking fraternity brother at a small but excellent southern college. His uncontrolled drinking had come to the attention of college administrators; he had been arrested for driving while drunk. Even so, Walter did fairly well in school. When Walter was home his father would take an opportunity to "talk some sense into the boy." Most of the time, though, the family never talked about Walter's "problem."

Then there was daughter Stacy, 13. She was strikingly beautiful—and knew it. Living up to the nickname, "Princess," which her father had given her years ago, Stacy was demanding and dramatic. She got a lot of attention from her parents, who avoided her tantrums by giving her what she wanted. They figured she would grow out of her adolescent testiness.

The lady of the house was Eleanor, Michael's mother. Everything about her bespoke perfection—her decorating, manners, personal style, and entertaining. She gave hours of service through the Junior League to worthwhile causes, displaying a gift for leadership. She also managed to get in some sets of tennis during her busy week, and participated in a women's Bible study at church.

As the family members grew older, they spent less time together. Grady's business was extremely demanding in an economically volatile time, and when he was home he seemed preoccupied with work. In the past he had taken his boys to sports events or on fishing trips, but since Michael was the only son at home now, Grady hadn't done anything like that recently.

The busier the parents became, the more Stacy demanded their attention. Michael, on the other hand, was an agreeable guy, and didn't cause any trouble. His parents appreciated what "a fine boy" he was, and often said so in front of guests. They did not say it as much to him—not because they didn't love him, but because they found it uncomfortable to talk about their feelings within the family. It was—well, embarrassing. But they did their best to provide all the material things their children needed.

Mom and Dad don't know a thing about how I feel, Michael had written one day in his journal. *They give me everything except the things I really need—love and time and a chance to talk with them. I feel so lonely. This isn't a home I live in—it's a neat little hotel. I feel so lonely sometimes.*

Another time he wrote, *I guess I'm the perfect kid—one who doesn't cause a lot of trouble or make a lot of noise. Sometimes I think that I'm going to make a big scene just once to see if anybody cares at all. Are you listening, world?*

During the past year, Michael had found someone who cared about him. She was Ashleigh, his first real girlfriend. They had been friends during the first three years of high school; Ashleigh, a cheerleader and member of the tennis team, ran with the "jocks." Many of Michael's male friends felt he'd really "scored" when he and Ashleigh started going together.

Michael and Ashleigh spent a lot of time together listening to music and studying. They went to school events, to movies, to the mall. Ashleigh was more outgoing and usually had the ideas for socializing; Michael was happy if the two of them just spent time talking. She was the first person Michael had ever opened up to, sharing his deepest life. And by the entries in Michael's journal, it was clear that he thought Ashleigh and their relationship were too good to be true.

As the relationship developed, Michael's male friends had begun to press him on whether he and Ashleigh had "gone all the way." His replies were always good-natured but vague. It wasn't until New Year's Day that they became sexually involved.

Soon after that the relationship began to change. Ashleigh pulled back, saying they were getting too deep. She needed room to breathe. Michael was bewildered, and tried harder to spend time with her. *I'm so scared that I'm going to lose Ashleigh,* Michael wrote one day, *and I don't know how to tell her, because she'll just want me less. I'm scared—she's the only one in the world who loves me.*

In March Ashleigh told Michael that she didn't want to go steady any longer. No, it wasn't another guy, she said. She just needed to be free. Michael was crushed. *I just don't know how I am going to live,* he wrote. He made the best of a bad situation with his friends. They were sympathetic for about a week, as Michael observed in one of his entries.

What no one knew was that Michael was obsessed with Ashleigh and what she had done. He seemed more and more remote to his friends. His teachers, who had never heard much in class from him, heard even less. His grades took a plunge.

He hardly ate—but no one really noticed, since the family didn't eat together often. Once, when they did, his parents observed that he wasn't eating much. He told them he wasn't hungry, that he was sorry.

"Sorry for what?" his mother asked.

"Sorry for everything," he answered as he left the table. Later in the evening, his father went to Michael's room to find the boy listening to music through headphones, staring vacantly.

After getting Michael's attention, his father asked what was wrong. "I don't want to talk about it," Michael answered.

"Is the problem that Ashleigh girl?" his father asked.

"I said, I don't want to talk about it."

"Son, sometimes that happens. But you'll get over it. There are a lot of girls out there who would like a boy like you. Just wait and see! You're a fine boy, Michael. Don't let it get you down. You've got to keep those grades up for school in the fall. Just keep at it, son," his father concluded.

Michael nodded. "Yes, sir. Now, could you leave me alone?"

When the outdoor track season began at the beginning of April, Michael's performance wasn't up to par. That was partly because he wasn't eating right, but mostly because he just wasn't interested. His coach gave him some encouragement and hints on improving his times, but with every losing race Michael felt worse.

In mid-April Michael went to the coach and said that he didn't want to race for a while. When the coach asked why, Michael said he needed to give attention to his grades—which were indeed getting worse. The coach accepted that reason, and assured Michael that he was welcome back any time. "I'm not sure I can come back," said Michael as he left.

Nobody cares if I'm here or not, Michael wrote in his journal. *It really doesn't matter anymore. I really don't matter. So why am I living?*

Michael's behavior grew more erratic. He couldn't get to sleep at night, and sometimes couldn't get out of bed in time to make it to school. He missed classes here and there so that he could go outside to sit—but never too often to arouse the suspicion of the administration. He spent less and less time with his friends.

One morning Michael told one of his friends, "I'm not going to be around soon." His friend asked whether he was moving. Michael said, "Yes—to a real nice place." He seemed happy. By lunchtime the word had spread, and his buddies asked him where he was going. "I don't know exactly. All I know is that it's really nice. You guys have been great. It's going to be really soon. I hope the track team can win without me."

So that afternoon, at the end of April, Michael walked home. He had written some notes during last period math class and stuck them in his binder. He walked up the drive to his house. The garage was open and empty. He knew his mother would not be back from the city tutoring program until late in the afternoon. Stacy was at a friend's house for dinner. His father was in London negotiating a construction project. Michael was all alone in the quiet of the house.

He placed a note in the crack of the door leading from the garage to the house, and another on the kitchen table. He left a note on Stacy's bed, and two sealed envelopes, one to each of his brothers. He put his school folders in a neat stack on his desk, put an album in his compact disc player, and went to his parents' bedroom where he knew his father kept a pistol hidden.

He brought the pistol and a bullet to his room, loaded the gun, lay on his bed, and raised the gun to his mouth. As the musicians sang, "Can you hear me calling?" he pulled the trigger.

When Eleanor opened the door from the garage to the house late that afternoon, she saw a note fall. She picked it up, jostling her bag of groceries. She put the groceries on the kitchen counter and, hearing some music from Michael's room, called, "Hey, Michael, how was school today?" She opened the note and read:

Dear Mom:
Don't go in my bedroom. It's awful, but I didn't know any
other way. I love you.
Michael
P.S. Read the note on the kitchen table. Call Dad right away.

"Michael?" she yelled. "Michael, are you all right?" Eleanor ran to the bedroom and recoiled at what she found. "Michael!" she shrieked.

Seeing blood everywhere, she ran back to the kitchen and called for the paramedics. They arrived in just a couple of minutes. Eleanor could not go back to the bedroom. As she recalled later, "It was like a chill I have never known before, like something evil there."

The paramedics rushed in and cursed under their breaths when they found Michael's body. There was no pulse, no blood pressure. One of the paramedics began to mop up some of the blood while the other radioed for the police and took Eleanor to the family room. A neighbor came running over to offer help.

The police came, snapped pictures, took the weapon, and called the family's pastor at home. He arrived as the paramedics pulled away with Michael's body, en route to the morgue for an autopsy and investigation.

Eleanor and the pastor called Grady in London. Speaking in a shaky voice but trying hard to be in charge, Grady said he would take the next flight home—which wouldn't get him there for at least 14 hours. Calling Stacy next, Eleanor told the girl to stay where she was for the moment.

Only later in the evening, when a couple of close friends had come over to help clean up the mess as well as they could, did Eleanor find Michael's letter on the kitchen table. It read,

Dear Mom and Dad:
I'm really sorry. I didn't want to hurt you, but I didn't know
what else to do. Nobody really cares about me, and I can't live
without someone who could love me. And you thought Ashleigh
was just another girlfriend. (Smile.) Tell her I love her always
and not to worry about me. I have notes to Princess and to
Grady and Walter, too. Please be sure they get them. Maybe I'll
see you someday. I'm scared!
Love, Michael

Each of the other notes contained a sentence or so in which Michael said he loved and would miss the sibling to whom it was addressed.

The funeral was held early the next week. Over 500 people came, including most of Michael's classmates. The whole story was big news in the paper, and concerns were raised that other teens might now attempt suicide. During that year, however, none did.

Grady and Eleanor insisted they'd had no idea Michael felt as he did. Both entered marital counseling to deal with the trauma Michael's suicide caused their marriage. Yet even today they cannot understand why their "fine boy" would choose the suicide route.

Kim

Sometimes it is not at all clear what "snaps" in the person who commits suicide. Whatever the crisis, there is nothing in the person's self-esteem to support him or her through it. This was tragically true for Kim.

Kim was not a "bad" girl, but a troubled one from a troubled family. Her parents had divorced when she was very young, and her father had disappeared. Then her mother lived with a succession of boyfriends, finally settling on one whom she married when Kim was in junior high. The man never physically or emotionally abused Kim, but she did not like him at all; when her mother and stepfather went on their honeymoon, Kim ran away from her grandmother's house and was not found for three weeks.

After two further "breaks" from her house, Kim's mother decided with a social worker that perhaps Kim needed to be placed in some therapeutic environment—not a detention home, but a place in which Kim could be monitored and guarded. Her mother felt out of control. So Kim was assigned by the caseworker to a state youth home, where the girl went without protest. "I don't care," she said simply.

Kim's behavior was average in the youth home, but she had periods of anger and rebellion. The home workers and the therapist agreed that Kim had nothing profoundly wrong with her. She was mixed up, unhappy, from an unstable home situation, a girl without needed coping skills.

One December Kim was especially rebellious in her

sophomore English class at school, and at the youth home. Kim's mother made it clear to the caseworker that she felt unable to look after her daughter at home during Christmas: "I just don't know what we will all do." The caseworker agreed, believing that the rebellious behavior could stop if clear limits and consequences were defined for Kim. So, when Kim disobeyed a set of house rules near Christmas week, she was informed that she would not be able to go home for Christmas.

It was plain that Kim was disappointed. But she covered that emotion with a defiant "I don't care" attitude.

No one was prepared a couple of mornings later to find Kim hanging by a lamp cord in her closet. There was no note, no warning that Kim would turn her anger in on herself. That suicide was the first one in the youth home. Kim's legacy spread; there were three other attempts during the six months following her death. Kim's mother sued the home for neglect and malpractice.

Harold

As previously noted, the statistically most likely suicide candidate in America is a white male over age 65. Here is the story of one such man. It is a true but composite report, combining the experiences of several individuals so that their anonymity is protected. See whether you can understand this person's motivation to commit suicide, and where you might have intervened had you had the opportunity.

Harold and Dorothy had seen hard times in their lives, but they always said they grew stronger through such times. Sharing a vibrant faith, they gave every evidence of being a secure and happy couple who would relish their retirement together.

Harold had come up through the ranks of the factory where he had worked since finishing high school in an old suburb of a northern industrial city. He met Dorothy, then a waitress, in the coffee shop where he and his friends had dinner once a week. Soon Harold and Dorothy fell in love, were married, moved to a small apartment, and began a family. Later they moved into a small house in the factory district when the second of their six children was born. Early in their family life, Harold and Dorothy both accepted Christ into their lives, and since then had been active in the little church in their neighborhood. Their lives revolved around each other, the church, their family, his

28

work—and bowling, their single weekly luxury.

The factory work paid well, but was highly dependent on a stable economy. Because of his increasing seniority, Harold was in less and less danger of losing his job, though he had been furloughed without pay several times in his working life. He considered himself lucky to have work when so many others lost their jobs from time to time. Finally, after 45 years, at age 65, in accordance with company policy (though still vigorous and with abundant experience and wisdom), Harold retired. He wasn't sure what he was going to do with himself, since he had never cultivated a hobby and did very little volunteer work outside the church.

One evening, soon after Harold retired, Dorothy suddenly slumped in her chair. She was alert, but unable to talk or move. The paramedics rushed her to the hospital, where doctors were able to stabilize her condition and put her into intensive care. The preliminary diagnosis: Dorothy had suffered a massive stroke. This was confirmed during the next few days while Dorothy slipped in and out of consciousness. She gave no sign of hearing or recognizing anyone.

The doctors explained to Harold that Dorothy's stroke meant that she would be immobilized and unable to speak. If her condition could be stabilized during the next few days, there was some chance that she could make some recovery with physical therapy—though nothing was guaranteed.

But Dorothy's condition worsened. Ten days after suffering her stroke, she died due to a blood clot in her brain. Harold and his two sons were at Dorothy's side when she stopped breathing and the doctors removed life supports.

The days that followed were a blur—the funeral, the papers to file for benefits, the cleaning of the apartment, the removal of Dorothy's clothing from her closet . . . Harold seemed lost in a daze. The woman to whom he had been married for nearly 50 years was gone.

Harold had always been quiet, not one for groups nor for sharing his feelings. Now he withdrew even more. His sons became concerned when he clearly was not taking care of himself; he was unshaven and rumpled-looking, both out of character. He was not eating well, and wanted to sleep during the day. He also grew increasingly remote and did not want to talk.

His sons and their families did not know how to break

through this barrier of grief. And their lives were busy; they regularly checked on Harold, but could only do so much. Harold would have to do some things to help himself, too.

Meanwhile, Harold could hardly express his feelings of lostness, hopelessness, and fear. He was so lonely for Dorothy, for her presence, her companionship, her stability. He wanted so much to be with her.

The thought dawned on him that maybe he could indeed be with her. *My life is over,* he began to think. *I don't want to be a burden to my children, and I can't stand not being with Dorothy. If she can't be with me, then I'll go to be with her.*

Harold put his financial affairs in order, and made sure his sons understood what he wanted done "when I die." It didn't occur to Harold's sons that he might be referring to an impending, planned death. After all, he was an older man, and older men do put their affairs in order.

Late one evening, nearly nine months after Dorothy died, Harold climbed into his car. He had written notes telling each of his sons that he loved them and their families, and that he was pleased that his financial affairs were all straight. He was feeling better than he had in some months, he wrote, and looked forward to brighter days ahead. He drove to the post office and mailed the letters.

His car was found at the bottom of a nearby lake two days later. He was inside, still strapped in the seat. His death was ruled "accidental" by the county coroner. His sons wanted to believe this judgment, but they knew better.

Alex

Wondering what I was going to find, I pulled into the driveway of the comfortable-looking suburban home. All I knew was that the husband of the woman who lived here had committed suicide just hours before. Neither the woman nor her husband were part of our congregation.

"I'm Pastor Throop," I told the fortyish woman who answered the door.

"I'm Marge. Who called you? Where are you from?" I explained that a friend of hers had called me. She seemed reassured and invited me in.

Marge took me to the family room and pointed at a large, black spot on the carpet. "That's where Alex shot himself." She sat down with a moan. "I just can't understand why he did it. Why would a man who had so much going for him do that? It's so stupid!"

I asked whether Alex had left a note. No, she said. But recently he had been quieter, more withdrawn than usual. He'd had some problems at work, where he was a loan officer for a suburban bank.

"Was he in some sort of trouble there, do you think?" I asked. She said no. The bank had told her Alex had a clean report—but he hadn't been producing loan income anywhere near the level they wanted. So he had been under some pressure. Marge wondered whether that pressure had caused him to crack.

"There was no warning, none at all." She shook her head. "And then to find him when I returned home from school. I'll never forget the scene." She shivered as she spoke.

Next day Marge and I began to plan the funeral. She chose Revelation 7:9-17 as the Scripture for the service. I based my message on that passage.

In the days after the funeral, I kept a close eye on Marge. As her shock slowly cleared away, she was able to piece together the truth about the tragedy. Previously hidden facts came to light: Alex's father had committed suicide when Alex was in college; Alex had purchased a gun a couple of months before the suicide; he had said one or two things in passing about his father's suicide, something he had rarely done in 12 years of marriage; and Alex had blamed himself for the trouble he was having on his job, feeling he simply couldn't cut it.

Marge joined a support group for survivors of suicide victims. A well-run program sponsored by our community hospital, it served as a transition point for people trying to make sense out of senseless and tragic events.

For several months Marge found it difficult to come to church. The memory of the funeral was still very much with her. More importantly, she found herself feeling angry with God. "Don't ask me to make sense of this," she told me bluntly. "I just feel this way now." I assured Marge that this was very normal, and that the God I knew was certainly big enough to take it.

One hopeful event occurred a few weeks after the suicide. Marge asked me to conduct a house blessing, which is done with some frequency in my tradition. We come to a house, usually a new one, or one into which a family or single person has moved, and we pray for God's blessing in each room of the house. I agreed to do so.

On the appointed day, friends and relatives joined Marge for the blessing. I walked through each room of the home, praying with Marge for God's presence and protection. Others remained in the family room—where Alex had killed himself—and prayed quietly. I then returned to the family room and prayed that the house would be lifted from all oppression and degradation, that indeed it would be a house consecrated to the Lord. After some concluding prayers, there was a party. It was a joyous event, a new beginning.

Several family members, Marge included, pulled me aside before I left to tell me what a remarkable experience they'd had during the blessing. All had felt a sudden physical warmth and spiritual peace, as if a darkness and oppression had been lifted. I knew enough from God's Word and from pastoral experience confirming that Word to conclude that the bondage of sin and death had been broken in the household. Marge wrote me a note a couple of weeks after the blessing to say that she now was sleeping nights for the first time since the suicide.

Having moved away from that community, I have lost track of Marge. I want to think she has moved on with her life—never forgetting Alex, but freed from the terrible power of the memory of his suicide.

Marge always said she was a survivor, but I know that she was more. She was made new by the grace of God, learning in the difficult school of life that God does work all things to the good for those who love Him—and for those, I would guess, who earnestly try to love Him through one of life's greatest tragedies.

Why would a person take his or her own life, or attempt to do so? As seen in these case studies, suicide is a complex phenomenon with as many causes as there are victims. Yet there are general guidelines that can be useful to those who would help the suicidal person and her or his loved ones. In the next chapter we will begin to explore those guidelines by dealing with questions that are commonly asked by those who would help the suicidal and their families.

CHAPTER THREE

QUESTIONS HELPERS ASK

H OW CAN YOU HELP THOSE WITH SUICIDAL TENDENCIES? What about those who are left behind when a relative kills himself or herself?

Suicide is a crisis that generates many questions for victims and helpers alike. This chapter provides an overview of suicide intervention and prevention, using questions helpers often ask. You should find the answers useful as you begin to consider your role in dealing with this crisis.

What makes people suicidal?

As noted in the previous chapter, each case is unique. But the following causes seem to underlie most urges toward self-destruction:

1. *Psychological problems.* In a sense all suicidal people are grappling with psychological problems, but some have clearly definable illnesses which are out of control. *Depression*, strictly defined, is one cause of suicide. The depressed person may have a physical, organic, medical problem which can be addressed only with medication (and that rather inexactly). Out-of-control depression, whatever its cause, can lead to suicidal behavior. *Psychosis* is another psychological factor. A psychotic person may have a desire to inflict harm on himself or herself.

2. *Intense psychological pain.* Psychologist Edwin Shneidman, in an article entitled, "At the Point of No Return" (*Psychology Today*, March 1987) describes a suicidal woman who jumped from a building. She survived to give this account of her decision to leap:

"I was so desperate. I felt, my God, I couldn't face this thing. Everything was like a terrible whirlpool of confusion. And I thought to myself: There's only one thing to do. I just have to lose consciousness. That's the only way to get away from it. The only way to lose consciousness, I thought, was to jump off something good and high. . . .

33

"I just walked until I found this open staircase. As soon as I saw it, I made a beeline right up to it. And then I got to the fifth floor and everything just got very dark all of a sudden, and all I could see was this balcony. Everything around it just blacked out. It was just like a circle.

"I climbed over it and then I just let go. I was so desperate. Just desperation, and the horribleness and the quietness of it. There was no sound. And I sort of went into slow motion as I climbed over the balcony. I let go and it was like I was floating. I blacked out. I don't remember any part of the fall."

This woman wanted to escape, to find relief from the intense pain she felt. The same is true of two suicidants whose stories were told in Chapter 2: "Michael," the heartbroken teenage boy, and "Harold," the elderly man who could not bear life without his wife. Where there is such intense pain, some want to escape it; they feel unable to endure it.

3. *Low self-esteem.* A key factor in the suicidal person's thinking is that he or she is truly worthless. A core of self-respect or self-valuation simply is not there. Perhaps it never had a chance to form because the parent or parents did not shape it, or damaged it, in the child's early years. The suicidal person believes that her or his life is completely dispensable. Suicide is an act of self-hatred and self-pity.

4. *Powerlessness and hopelessness.* The suicidal person believes there is no way to change his or her situation in life. The problems he or she faces are insurmountable; nothing can be done to alter the circumstances. As Edwin Shneidman writes, "Suicidal individuals think of only two alternatives: a total solution or a total cessation. All other options have been driven out by desperation and pain." The most dangerous word in the suicidal person's vocabulary, he notes, is the word "only." Death is the "only" choice.

I remember clearly how true this was for me. When I nearly attempted suicide in my early teens, my parents had moved our family just as I was establishing friendships and finding direction. There was nothing I could say or do to prevent the move. I was powerless, or felt that way. After all, who would listen to a teenager's opinion? I see with hindsight that there were compelling reasons to move, but at the time I did not have the benefit of perspective and patience. Feeling alone, isolated, my life out of control, I saw no alternative other than ending it all. It was better, I thought, than living life without any choice or any say.

5. *Lack of coping skills.* The suicidal person has not learned to deal well with setbacks or frustrations that many of us are able to move through. Emerging bruised but wiser from difficulty—that simply is impossible for many suicidal people to imagine. Their frustration, anger, shame, and pain build until the pressure seems too great to take.

It is no wonder that a lack of coping skills contributes heavily to suicide in our society. In the last half of the 20th century, these skills have been harder to teach and to learn. Today we tend to think that problems can be solved instantly, often by science and technology. Our teens are at risk because they have not learned to wait, to do without, to stick with relationships and commitments, and to live in a future that cannot guarantee them more and better. Many adults have not learned skills for coping, either. They are not prepared to trust in God's provision and care.

6. *Lack of faith.* Related to all these factors is a fundamental reason for suicide—a lack of faith. The suicidal person may have heard about God's love and care through the love and care of others, but that is not enough. The missing link in the suicidal person's life is a lack of faith, a belief that God really is there for him or her. Suicide is the ultimate act of selfishness, declaring that the individual will be in charge of his or her own life and destiny, and that such a life is hopeless—without God and without love.

Does this mean Christians don't commit suicide?

I wish that were true. It's not. While there are no statistics on this available, I can speak from my own ministry, as well as ministries of my peers. Some of the most stalwart church members commit suicide, or attempt it. A Christian can believe fervently that Christ is the answer to life's tough problems, but sometimes feel overwhelmed by those problems. Some even come to believe that, by committing suicide, they will escape to the comfort of Jesus and finally be free.

How can a helper begin to intervene in a suicidal person's life?

The minister, lay counselor, or psychologist must be there for the suicidal person first of all as a friend. That is the one thing a suicidal person desperately needs—a friend. The person may reject your friendship, but it is essential that if you know a person thinking about suicide, you stick with the person—checking on him or her regularly, listening more than talking, praying more than advising.

Are there any specific responsibilities I have to a suicidal person?

Yes! In nearly all states, if you know of someone who is threatening to commit suicide and you are providing advice and counsel, you must seek out professional help for the person. You are legally liable to intervene. More information on this point will be provided in Chapter 7. If you know someone who clearly is going to take her or his own life, call the police, get the person to a mental health center, or bring her or him to a hospital emergency room. Do not leave the person alone.

How would I know whether someone might commit suicide?

As noted in the first chapter, 80 percent of all suicides are preceded by a warning of some kind. So there may well be clues that any careful listener would pick up—phrases such as, "It would be better if I were gone," "Life is just not worth living any more," or, "I'm not going to be around much longer."

Be on the lookout for significant changes in behavior, too. If a normally well-adjusted person becomes deeply depressed, you are being a good friend if you inquire about what is wrong. Likewise, if someone who has been deeply depressed seems suddenly very cheerful, don't be fooled or relieved. The normal pattern of recovery is like that of a hurricane. You go through a stormy time, and then the calm and sunshine of the eye comes. But anyone who has been through a hurricane knows that there is more storm coming. So it is with depression—there is gradual recovery, with few miraculous healings.

Be especially careful if the person once depressed and now cheerful talks about "moving away" or being "glad for the peace" and the like. These can be signs that the person has made a decision to commit suicide and is at peace with this way out of the problems and the unbearable sadness he or she is experiencing. The suicidal person may only be waiting for the moment when he or she can go through with the plan.

Beware of sudden mood changes—silence, withdrawal, distraction, and the like. If a person who never has been interested in guns suddenly buys one, that could be a warning sign. If someone is pressing to "get things in order," particularly after experiencing a tragic event, he or she should be monitored. An example: a teenager who, after a period of sadness and withdrawal, starts to give things away to family members or friends.

Sometimes a person will say bluntly that he or she is thinking of committing suicide. This is not a time to crack jokes to cheer the person up, or to comment on how silly that sounds, or to give the person a pat on the back and a hearty "Things can't be that bad." To the suicidal person, things *are* that bad. Take such a threat seriously. Ask questions gently to see whether the person is getting any kind of help or has told anyone else.

In a caring way, find out whether the person has any specific plans for carrying out this currently vague threat. Remember that a person who has told you that he or she wants to commit suicide generally has thought about how to do it, and is crying out for your help *not* to do it. The more specific the plan, the greater the likelihood that the suicide will be attempted.

In my own case years ago, had anyone asked me about my suicide plans I would have described them in some detail. I had them all figured out. Later I learned that this fascination with the detail of taking one's own life is part of the terrible, twisted logic in a suicidal person's mind.

Then there was the case of Mary, a woman who called me one evening. She was obviously upset. Her speech was halting as she said, "I have a bottle of sleeping pills in my hand."

"Why are you telling me this?" I asked.

"Well, I'm going to take them," she said.

"All of them?"

"Yes."

"How many are there?"

"Fifty-three."

"Do you have anything else?"

"Yes. Some vodka."

"Is anyone else there?"

"No, Jim [her husband] is on a business trip, and the children are gone for the evening at a friend's house."

"Mary," I said, "don't do a thing till I get there! Do you understand?"

She said she did. I raced over and discovered that, thank God, she had listened to me.

It was clear that Mary had planned her own death. Because everything was so carefully arranged, I knew there was a very grave risk that she would commit suicide.

To repeat: If you know someone is intent on killing himself or herself, you *must* intervene. And if the person has attempted suicide before, it is likely that he or she will attempt again. Do not dismiss suicide threats.

Why try to prevent suicide? After all, shouldn't a person be free to choose to end his or her own life?

A surprising number of people think this way. As already mentioned, you have a legal obligation to report a likely suicide whether you agree with the law or not.

The theological problem with this question will be addressed in Chapter 6. For now, let us note that while there may be a logic to suicide and suicidal behavior, it is a twisted logic. Even the suicidal person, to whom self-inflicted death seems the only course, feels some ambivalence. Wanting to go through with it because there appears to be no other choice, he or she also *doesn't* want to go through with it.

When I intervene, what should I do?

If the suicidal person is in extreme danger, call the police right away. Let them take the necessary action to save the person's life.

In a less critical situation, make a referral. This is true if you are a friend, but also if you are a lay counselor or a member of the clergy. Suicidal persons need attention from mental health professionals who have the training and skills for effective intervention. Your local mental health department can be helpful here. If you are a friend, your first phone call may be to your minister or priest for advice and counsel.

If possible, the mental health professional should be a Christian. The first priority, though, is for the suicidal person to get the best-trained care available, especially for a medical as well as a psychological evaluation. As already noted, depression can have organic or physical causes. Allergic reactions and thyroid problems, for example, can be agents in depression. A mental health professional should have the skills to make this evaluation.

It is important to have spiritual advice and guidance, too. The suicidal person needs to be aware of God's love and care for him or her. He or she needs to be prayed for and upheld by the Body. There is a real place for prayer and spiritual counsel and direction, and it should be provided in tandem with psychological treatment.

I certainly believe in the power of God to work wonders and miracles. I have known some of them myself. At the same time, I believe God gives us the responsibility to get the best care possible for our brothers and sisters, along with the best prayer and guidance we ourselves can offer. Unless you are a Christian mental health professional, please do not attempt to counsel and treat out of your range of training and education. You can be the best friend possible to the suicidal person, and that's plenty right there!

I've been urging a suicidal person to see a counselor, but the person is afraid. What can I tell the person to ease his fears?

You could try something like this:

"It's nothing to be afraid of. The counselor will ask you to give a history of your health, ask you to describe your feelings, and to describe whatever plans you may have to follow through on your feelings. He or she will want to gauge the seriousness of your intent. If the counselor does think you're serious, he or she may commit you to a mental health facility for your protection.

"If that happens, you will be held for an indeterminate period of time to be evaluated and watched for signs of illness (and wellness). You will receive a medical and psychological exam from a psychiatrist. If you seem particularly nervous or upset, some sedative medication may be prescribed until the episode of anxiety or outburst passes."

If the suicidal person wants your assurance that he or she could leave the mental health facility at will, explain that this is not the case. A person committed to a mental health facility by a professional or by the police loses his or her civil rights and is placed under the care of the facility's staff. Only when staff members believe that the threat to the person's life and health has passed will they release him or her. The person will be released to the care of someone who can be responsible for him or her until recovery from being suicidal begins.

My friend has attempted suicide and survived. What should I do? What should I say?

Be a friend. Visit the person in the hospital. True, a mental health unit can be a frightening place if you've never been in one before, but make the effort (and be sure to call ahead for visiting policies). Include the person in your prayers when you are not able to visit—and when you are.

Don't be surprised if the person isn't in the mood to talk. Sometimes a would-be suicidant is sedated or otherwise drugged and can't think clearly, or is still feeling the effects of the suicide instrument.

When the effects of the drugs wear off, or as healing from self-inflicted injuries has progressed, the person may exhibit a lot of anger. He or she is ashamed because the attempt did not succeed. Perhaps there is some permanent physical damage which will serve as a constant reminder of a botched attempt. The psychological pain still is present and the life situation is not altered. So the person may tell you to go away—and you may have to. But you need to reassure the person that you are there, and that you really do love him or her. You may need to do a lot more listening than talking. If you do have to leave at the person's angry insistence, let him or her know that you will be back.

Don't beat around the bush about the suicide attempt. You and the suicidal person both know why he or she is recovering. The worst thing is to pretend that nothing happened. But don't dwell on the subject, either. Just acknowledge the fact of the attempt and talk about other aspects of life as well. The suicidal person needs to be brought into the flow of living. Talk about the future, too, with the person as part of it.

Should I pray with the suicidal person?

Yes, if you want to. But don't be surprised if your attempts are met with anger or some other rebuff. If you are praying in the hope of preventing an attempt, be prepared to act responsibly in concert with your prayer. It's not enough to pray and figure that God will take care of it—a kind of "name it and claim it" style of prayer. If the person does commit suicide anyway—and that has happened—the courts will not consider your prayer a form of intervention and treatment.

After unsuccessfully attempting suicide, a person may be

ready for prayer and godly direction. Spiritual rehabilitation is needed—and the person probably knows this deep down—but he or she also needs to know of God's grace and forgiveness and love. When you pray, thank God that He has given the person another chance at life, and that He is sovereign and loving and has a good plan for this child of His. Pray also for the Spirit of God to heal the person inwardly and outwardly.

Please be merciful, however, and do not press the person for an immediate decision to follow Jesus. It is also unhelpful to tell the person that he or she is a sinner who needs to repent of this ungodly act of attempting suicide. I've seen and heard this happen, and it is "guerilla Christianity" of the worst kind. The suicidal individual already feels deeply alienated from God, is keenly aware of his or her sinfulness and worthlessness, and *knows* that he or she needs a Savior from this personal morass. The problem is, how can he or she make the step? I would try to develop a loving relationship in which the person can be led to a loving Lord whom he or she needs for life itself. Love, don't lecture the suicidal person into a living relationship with Jesus Christ.

How can I help the suicidal person change his or her twisted logic?

The person needs perspective and hope. You can help by showing how to broaden his or her range of options and perspective.

The suicidal person sees life completely in either/or terms. Either he or she must go on with a painful life, or die. There are no other options.

I once met with a man who was having trouble in his small business. He was nearly bankrupt due to bad judgment and bad timing. Increasingly depressed, he had fallen into a downward spiral in which he felt that he was failing not only in this enterprise, but in everything. He believed he was a bad businessman, a bad husband and father, a worthless servant of God—all because he was failing at his business venture. A sense of shame and self-loathing had filled him. He had become convinced that committing suicide was the only choice that made any sense. He would get out of business and sever his family ties, making sure that family members were "taken care of." Then he would end it all—quietly, by himself.

When I deduced his plans I went to him. He was surprised,

flustered, and not a little angry when I bluntly told him that I knew what he had been thinking. Impressed with my directness, he began to tell me his story. He told me that he had no choice. He had to commit suicide.

I took a kind of inventory with him. What was the absolutely worst thing that could happen to him? He would go bankrupt and lose everything, he answered. And then what? He could never, ever get a start again in business. *Everyone* would know what an utter failure he had been.

Did that mean he could never work again? No, he said. Then he thought and said, well, no, at least not in the work he had been accustomed to.

But could he work at *something?* Well, yes. Already there was a glimmer that *something* else was possible in his life. The crack in the door marked "No Options" had appeared. This was the beginning of a long journey back to hope and healing.

Whether you are a friend or a professional, you can use this logical approach. It is not enough by itself, but it is a vital element in the healing process.

How closely should the suicidal person be monitored?

If the person has given evidence of a clear plan of suicide or has made a recent attempt at it, he or she must be watched very closely until professional help can be obtained or the person is committed (generally only temporarily) to an institution. If the person is talking about suicide only in general terms, it is usually more appropriate to check in with the person on a daily basis until he or she is in contact with a helping professional.

What about caring for the person after an attempt?

If the person is likely to return to a situation which would only put him or her in a suicidal state again, you might find the person another place to live for a while. Be sure to consult the professional helper on this matter.

Call the person regularly to ask, "How are you coming along?" The suicidal person needs to know that he or she has not been rejected further because of the attempt.

Be sure that the person takes his or her medication, if that is part of the treatment. Many people mistakenly disregard medication once they start feeling better.

How likely is it that the person might try again to commit suicide?

Statistically the likelihood is small within the first year or two of the initial attempt. In one study, only 10.7 percent of those who attempted suicide attempted it again—even in 35 years. But I must stress that there are always exceptions to the pattern.

A person recovering from a suicide attempt may wonder whether he or she will have more episodes of suicidal thinking in the future. You might answer such a question along these lines:

"It certainly is possible that you would have these feelings again. The goal of therapy or counseling is to help you find alternatives in working out problems—alternatives that really help to solve the problems, which suicide never does. So, when confronting future crises—and there will be crises—if you've found an alternative to suicidal thinking, you'll know you have the inner resources to deal with the problem."

What can be done for the family of a person who attempts suicide?

When a family member attempts suicide, the family pattern is of course thrown out of balance. Some counselors talk about a family system, in which each person has an important part to play in the way the family lives. Often the person attempting or committing suicide is crying for help in a difficult family setting. That's why the family of the suicidal person often enters "family therapy." The suicidal person is not seen as an isolated circumstance or problem, but as part of a larger unit in trouble. This kind of counseling can bring a greater sense of stability to family life, which enables the suicidal person to think about options for living, rather than a single way to escape.

Families respond differently to suicide attempts in their midst. Some heed the cry for help. Others undertake a conspiracy of silence. Still others totally avoid the problem. The latter is especially true of, but not limited to, those whose elderly parents attempt suicide.

In one case, a 16-year-old honors student and top athlete shot himself to death because he could no longer cope with his home life. He had been coming home daily to an unemployed, alcoholic father, and a mother who dealt with problems by ignoring them. Even as he lay dying in the emergency room of the local hospital, his parents could find no reason why their son might kill himself. They flatly refused to believe that suicide was the cause of death.

By the grace of God, some families do find themselves shocked into action. They learn that, even though they never deliberately drove a son to the brink of death or a daughter to despair, or neglected a mother out of spite or a father out of forgetfulness, there was something very wrong in their communication and problem-solving abilities. As a pastor, I have been constantly amazed at how little families *really* communicate.

How can I approach a family in which someone has committed suicide?

You will have to gauge first whether family members have come to grips with the notion that one of their own has committed suicide. Some family members never admit that suicide was the cause—even in the face of compelling evidence.

But the initial reaction is that of any family experiencing the sudden death of a loved one. There is shock, numbness. Some have described this feeling as "floating in space" or "being in another world." This is a biological response to immense stimuli.

Your first helping strategy should simply be *presence*. You need to be available in practical ways, helping to clean up, seeing that other family members are cared for, providing transportation, assisting in the preparation of what seem to be innumerable forms and reports.

What should I expect to find if I clean up?

Since this is a blunt question, here are blunt answers. If the person used a gun, you may expect to find blood—pints and pints of it, the exact amount depending on where the wound was inflicted. This is one of the most repugnant sights you will ever have to see. Even war veterans who have seen a lot of blood shrink from the sight. Then there's the stench. If there is carpeting in the room, you will probably help to tear it up rather than try to clean it. It is one of the single greatest acts of Christian charity, I'm convinced.

If the person took drugs, such as sleeping pills, or poisons, such as cyanide, you will have excrement to deal with. Sometimes people (especially women, in Western culture) ingest drugs or poisons because they do not mar the features. But drugs and poisons do relax the muscles governing bodily functions.

Do suicide victims have regular funerals and Christian burials?

Yes. The theological dimensions of this question will be discussed in more detail in Chapter 6. Suffice it to say for now that suicide victims, in nearly every Christian tradition, are granted Christian burial. How services are handled will be the decision of family members in consultation with the pastor. But the suicide victim is nearly always treated with Christian dignity and charity. The service is an important opportunity for people to come to terms with self-inflicted death and the impulse human beings seem to have to destroy themselves.

What can I say at such a service?

Speaking for myself, I would preach a sermon to help people interpret what God might be saying in this tragedy—how God might be present in this inexplicable event that is filled with wrenching grief for the survivors. This is a key time at which peoples' hearts and minds are wide open. They want answers, particularly to these two questions: Where is God in all of this? Why did God let this happen? The preacher is in a unique situation to speak words of God's comfort and hope in this tragedy.

What Bible texts could I use in a funeral sermon to help surviving family members and friends?

I would begin by focusing on the reality of what has happened. I would not avoid the word suicide, but would acknowledge it matter-of-factly. People won't listen to a word you say unless you are compassionately clear with them.

Then I would refer to a text like Isaiah 25:6-9 and talk about the fact that the Lord's salvation is near even now, and that God's work is to swallow up death forever, to forgive sin for good, and to wipe away tears and take away pain.

Or I would focus on Psalm 22, preaching on the power of forsakenness, yet persevering with David to say, "For he has not despised or disdained the suffering of the afflicted one; he has not hidden his face from him but has listened to his cry for help" (Ps. 22:24). Or I could turn to Psalm 130, and cry out with David, "Out of the depths I cry to you, O Lord; O Lord, hear my voice" (Ps. 130:1, 2a). Indeed, many psalms are rich preaching

45

territory for sermons dealing with suicide, for they speak to all those who grapple with pain. As mentioned at the beginning of this book, I once preached from Psalm 23 and was compelled to use suicide as an example of walking through the valley of the shadow of death.

One could also preach out of Ecclesiastes. Like the Teacher, many attending the funeral probably think that all is meaning-less; indeed, one in their midst concluded that and died. But the Christian lives in profound hope that, in Christ, God has brought meaning to life.

Jesus' death and resurrection are key elements of any hopeful preaching on the occasion of suicide. But hearers will have to be convinced by God's grace and power that the whole thing is not fraudulent; after all, the deceased would still be living if he or she had sufficient hope in Christ's resurrection.

Stories out of the gospels, such as Matthew 16:21-28, or Luke 6:46-49, or John 11:21-27, or John 14:1-6 all provide possibili-ties for interpreting God's Word in this tragedy. The apostle Paul provides notes on resurrection in I Corinthians 15. Hebrews 4:14-16 is a good text on the presence of the compassionate Christ, though a speaker would want to answer the question of why some—like the one who committed suicide—do not under-stand that Christ is able to sympathize with all our weaknesses (v. 15).

Should I talk about the fact that suicide is a sin?

If you want to judge, warn, or criticize those who would do such a terrible, sinful thing, you will want to put into perspective the fact that we all have sinned and fallen short of the glory of God. We are justified freely by His grace through the redemp-tion that came by Christ Jesus (Rom. 3:23, 24).

I wouldn't want to presume, but to rest on God's mercy. And that is what I would emphasize.

Family members want assurance that their loved one has not bought a first-class ticket to hell by committing suicide. At the very least, I remind them of God's merciful nature. Inside, I thank God that He is loving and just, and trust that He will desire the best for the ravaged soul who comes to Him with a pain concluded in suicide. See Chapter 6 for more on the theolo-gy of suicide.

How can I help the surviving family in the months after the suicide?

Those first months are cruel. As the reality of suicide begins to reach their hearts, many family members experience a wrenching within, a feeling of guilt and anger.

"Why didn't she tell me about the problem?" they may ask. Then the "if onlys" set in: "If only I had done a little more, listened more often, loved more clearly, then this wouldn't have happened." They wonder why the deceased took such an extreme measure when the problem, from their perspective, seems so workable, even transitory.

So you will have to listen as the pain comes pouring out. There is much grief to be suffered and worked through. There is a kind of pattern to it, which Elisabeth Kübler-Ross identified as she worked with terminally ill patients.

First, there is *denial*. "No, he did not commit suicide, it was only an accident." Some circumstances lend themselves more easily than others to this explanation. "He is not really dead, just gone away—so I'll keep the room exactly as it has been for when he comes home." Then there is the silent treatment: "We won't talk about the 'situation.'"

Next there is *anger*. The survivors are angry at the one who committed suicide for doing such a despicable thing, for causing them so much pain. There is anger in the family, and a lot of blaming for letting this tragedy occur. There is anger at others: The school counselors should have known better; the physician or psychologist could have diagnosed more carefully; the minister could have intervened; the police didn't come fast enough. The list could go on.

This anger is very real, and it is an attempt on the part of the survivors to make sense out of something senseless. Listen carefully and be present as a friend or counselor. This is a necessary, though not always rational, step.

Then there is *bargaining*. Usually the family member bargains with God. Sometimes he or she will plead for another chance with the other parent, or an opportunity to do right with another teen, or a chance for communication at a deeper level with another spouse. In exchange for what? Who can say? Sometimes the bargaining is irrational, designed to get another chance with the person who committed suicide. This step must be worked through, but one cannot stop here, tempting as it may be.

Then there is *depression*. The anger is turned inward, as is the blame. The reality of what has happened finally permeates a deep level of the soul. One we loved has died and is gone from this life, and we are left—in pain and lonely. This is true even if there was a problem in the former relationship, for somehow in the glow of grief the past doesn't seem quite so bad. Where the relationship is perceived to have been good, there is the depression of abandonment and rejection.

Finally, there is *acceptance*. Not everyone reaches this stage. Indeed, some people I know and have counseled have never moved past denial; they've never really accepted the fact that a suicide happened. It's just too painful for them. Others bravely move ahead, never forgetting the person who committed suicide but realizing that their lives must go on. They are indeed sadder but wiser. They make good counselors for peers, too.

As you listen to surviving family members, you can expect to hear parts of this pattern. The length of time it takes for a person to pass through all the stages varies, and not everyone experiences each stage.

What can I tell a family member who can't understand why his or her loved one committed suicide, and who is angry at God for allowing it?

The sad truth is that we may never understand why a person would be driven to the point of suicide. Often the real reasons are known only to the person who has died. Through counseling, however, the survivor may be able to make some peace with himself or herself and work through the immense grief.

As for being angry at God, you might share something like this with the person:

"The first thing to do is to be angry. God is big enough to take your anger, and He still loves you! It is very natural for a person, even a person of deep faith, to ask questions of God, to be angry at God. Just read the Book of Job for biblical evidence of this point of view.

"But it's one thing to be angry with God for letting this suicide happen, and quite another to blame God for it. This is the eternal tension between predestination and free will in human life. God has given all of us choices in life, to live for Him or to go our own way without Him. The suicidal person really is responsible for his act of suicide. God did not will that person's destruction.

God cannot be held responsible for that person's death. That person's death is clear evidence of the Fall, in which all of us participate, which leads to sin and death. Some bring death upon themselves naturally, others intentionally end their lives violently.

"So, yes, you can be angry at God for the senselessness of it all, the terrible power of human sin, and even for permitting the awfulness of human choice. Yet to be angry at God means that you still are in relationship with Him, which is your hope. For you also will find solace in His grace and hope for tomorrow. Only by His power can you go on with your life."

Do those who commit suicide think about how much they hurt those who are left behind?

Not too often, according to researchers. Remember that suicide is most often a form of escape from what is perceived to be unbearable pain. It is not primarily a means of hurting others, though it is frequently a way of sending a message and issuing a cry for help.

Suicide, by nature, is a very selfish act. The focus is on the self and its annihilation, not on what the completion of the act would do to others.

Sometimes the suicidal person clearly is angry, though, so there is some hurting involved. But there is enough ambivalence in many cases to suggest that the suicidal person wants to hurt so that something can be done to deal with the problem, not to inflict injury on others forever.

When someone attempts or commits suicide, what "message" could he or she be trying to send?

Here are some:

1. "Nobody cares about me." The suicidal person is deeply self-centered, and has "tunnel vision" about the way things really are. He or she may be surrounded by loved ones, but feels pain that is not receiving attention.

2. "They would be better off without me." The suicidal person may think she or he is the root of all family problems, not realizing what a complex system a family is. His or her coping skills are minimal. Escape is seen as the only solution to pain and trouble.

3. "If I'm not around, our financial (or marital or legal or fam-

ily) problems will be easier to solve." Again, the suicidal person feels that he or she is the root of trouble, and that the solution is for him or her to be gone. Ironically, if the problem is a financial one, those left behind are forced to pick up the pieces. This can be a crushing burden.

These are just three of several messages that the person attempting or committing suicide may be trying to send to loved ones. That message may be sent in a note, or it may not.

When possible, it can be constructive for friends and professionals to help discern reasons for a suicide. This enables loved ones to have some peace of mind, giving them a way to explain this awful event. It can also suggest changes they should make in other relationships.

I'm not a counselor, just a friend. Where can I send a suicidal person or surviving family member?

Some churches have sound and established pastoral counseling services using trained and professional staff, a number of whom are ordained as well. That is a place to begin, along with pastoral help. Many members of the clergy are able to help make referrals, though few are able to help significantly in the psychological area.

Many communities and counties have mental health services, often affiliated with a local hospital. These are tax-supported and have a responsibility to work with all who present themselves regardless of ability to pay for the service (though there will be some kind of charge).

Private psychologists and psychiatrists are able to handle many problems. Consult with your clergy about a recommendation and referral. Looking at the Yellow Pages of the phone book will not be enough, since you can't determine a psychologist's reputation in this way.

If the suicidal person is a student, the guidance office at his or her school may be helpful to you. For an elderly person, many communities have senior services which can make appropriate suggestions.

Finally, and sometimes most importantly, there are suicide hotlines and intervention services in many communities. The Samaritans are an intervention organization that has many local chapters, particularly in urban areas. There are also a number of groups for suicide survivors; indeed, there is an organization by that name that has chapters in some communities. For details on hotlines and helping groups in your area, write to the American Association of Suicidology (see Bibliography for the address).

There was a teenage suicide in our area recently. Should we talk about it in our church, or ignore it so that other kids won't get the same idea?

When a teen commits suicide, parents, members of the clergy, helping professionals, and school officials must take the lead in addressing the concern. It is more important to take the lead in calming students and giving them perspective and balance than to go on as if nothing very significant happened. The student network will be working overtime with news of a peer's suicide.

Some psychologists and suicidologists talk of "suicide clusters" in communities. That is, there may be several suicides during a period of time in a certain community or school. This has been the case in Texas, Nebraska, Oregon, Illinois, and elsewhere. So effective, early intervention is crucial.

Honesty is crucial, too. To talk about suicide, coping with life's problems, and dealing with disappointment does not in itself encourage another to take his or her own life. Indeed, this kind of discussion immeasurably helps people to cope. They think, *Someone knows what I'm feeling. I'm not the only one.*

Talking about suicide in a way that romanticizes it, or focuses on the act or the person, can give unhealthy encouragement to those who are already contemplating the act. But talking about it and offering a way out lessens the incidence. Silence alone kills.

What about group suicides?

Fortunately, mass suicides such as the one involving 900 followers of Jim Jones in Jonestown, Guyana happen very rarely. But deaths involving a few teens who have made "suicide pacts" occur with greater frequency. In Tennessee, for example, four girls recently agreed to commit suicide. Fortunately, an adult learned of their plans and the girls were gently confronted. They said they had agreed to kill themselves "on a dare"!

Two girls in suburban Chicago went through with their plans; tragically, they were successful. It is essential that, where there is evidence of a pact, intervention is swift.

When those who commit suicide give specific instructions on

51

how to handle their funerals, should those wishes be respected?

Not necessarily. If the instructions are followed, the survivors can be manipulated by a logical, yet sick mind. Four teens who committed suicide at the same time in New Jersey wanted to be buried together in a common plot after a common funeral. The school officials, parents, clergy, and town officials wisely did not follow this direction.

Playing special tapes, reading notes, playing music the person wanted at the funeral—these should be avoided. The suicide victim should no longer be allowed to be at the center of his or her world.

CHAPTER FOUR

COUNSELING

ARE YOU QUALIFIED TO COUNSEL A SUICIDAL PERSON? IF SO, what patterns can you use? Whether you are a pastor or a professional therapist, this chapter can help you increase your effectiveness—and, just as importantly, remind you of your limitations.

Some Basic Assumptions

In writing this chapter, I am assuming that you work from a Christian perspective. You counsel out of a Christian value system and from your own deep Christian commitment.

I also assume that you have had some kind of training. It is a very dangerous thing to play psychiatrist when facing so difficult a problem as suicide.

This raises an important question: Must you be a psychologically-trained professional to counsel the suicidal? There is no absolute answer to this question. After all, even people under professional care sometimes commit suicide; a Ph.D. does not come with a warranty against failure. And most states do not have licensing requirements for someone to hang out a shingle with the word "counselor" or "therapist" on it.

You must be aware, however, that a relatively untrained person runs added risks in counseling the suicidal. If the family of a suicidant sues a counselor for negligence, and if the case comes to court, the court will look carefully at the counselor's qualifications in determining responsibility and liability. One element the court will consider is educational training. A Ph.D. or an M.D. from a recognized university will carry much more weight than an eight-week, non-certificate training seminar at a local church.

A rule of thumb, then, would be this: If you are not trained in a degreed program at a recognized educational institution, you can counsel with someone who is suicidal only as long as you are clear in your own mind that the person is not in imminent danger of self-harm. If the person shows the slightest inclination to self-harm, then you should let a degreed professional take over. This places the responsibility for care in the hands of someone with specific and disciplined training, and reduces the risk of legal action should the intervention fail.

Is the average pastor qualified to counsel the suicidal? In some Bible colleges and seminaries, suicide is not even discussed in pastoral care classes. In my seminary, a single day was devoted to this and other crisis events. The average pastor, then, can go only so far in counseling a suicidal person. Even with more reflection and training than the average pastor might have, I generally have referred suicidal people to professional counselors and psychologists long before the counselees were in imminent danger of self-harm.

In providing this chapter's counseling suggestions, therefore, I assume that you are either a member of the clergy who has had some guidance in seminary on counseling and pastoral care, or a counselor, ordained or lay, with some formal training. I also assume that you are under supervision, or, at the very least, accountable to someone for your counseling method. Finally, I assume that you will refer a counselee to a licensed professional, particularly a psychiatrist, the moment it appears that the person's problem is beyond your expertise.

Suicide is too critical a condition to be left to an amateur psychologist to treat. A life hangs in the balance. I implore you to recognize your limitations as you deal with the suicidal person; a little humility goes a long way in this area.

Basic Counseling Patterns with the Suicidal

Dr. Edwin Shneidman, whose work has been quoted already in this book, is professor of thanatology at the University of California, Los Angeles, founder of the American Association of Suicidology, and author of three leading texts in the field. In his article, "At the Point of No Return" (*Psychology Today*, March 1987), Shneidman suggests that there are three primary traits of the suicidal person.

First, there is the *unbearable pain* of the suicidal person's psyche, from which the person desires to escape.

Second, there are *thwarted needs* of the suicidal person—for love, acceptance, forgiveness, trust, and security.

Third, there is the *constriction of options* in the suicidal person's thinking. He or she can think of no alternative or solution other than committing suicide.

It follows that a key element of counseling the suicidal is seeking to ease the pain by getting it into the open. The process is like setting a broken bone; one must mend the brokenness so that healing can begin.

The counselor should also help to provide for some of the person's basic needs. This will lead the counselor to be a friend, to demonstrate trustworthiness and steadfastness, and to give assurance that the counselee really will be okay.

The counselor will also want to broaden the person's sense of option or choice, to lead him or her to agree at some point that suicide is not the only solution, and not a good one.

What about the spiritual aspect of counseling the suicidal? There is a spiritual emptiness at the core of suicidal thinking, and here is where the Christian counselor can make a strong and positive contribution. But the counselor *must* deal with the life-threatening aspects of suicide first. There will be time to deal with the spiritual problems as long as the person is out of danger.

The person probably will not say, "I am suicidal because I am the center of my life, not Jesus Christ." But that is the case. In the course of counseling, the helper should not be reticent in bringing spiritual issues to the forefront. Only in Jesus Christ is there hope for those without hope, and help for those in despair. The Christian counselor's task will be, in part, to help restore—or build for the first time—solid spiritual foundations in the person's life.

Counselors should also keep in mind that suicide is not just an isolated phenomenon of the individual. We live in families, in community. The suicide attempt is a cry for help in a family or community.

The wise counselor will realize that, for healing to occur, the rest of the family or community will have to become involved. The counselor will engage in family therapy to get at the suicidal person's problems with communication and self-esteem, which probably exist in the rest of the family as well. For further reading on this approach, consult two books by Virginia Satir, dean of the "family therapy" school, published by Science and Behavior Books of Palo Alto, California. They are *Conjoint Family Therapy* (1967; for the professional) and *Peoplemaking*

(1972; for the professional and the family).

Counseling the Teenager

It seems so senseless for a teenager to kill himself or herself. After all, so many teen problems are transitory; so much life is ahead, and there is so much to live for.

Yet there is a mystery in maturation that allows for perspective, the long view, an ability to compare with past failures and successes. Many teens, even those who are well-adjusted or socially advanced, simply do not have the emotional maturity, particularly in early adolescence, to see the larger picture. Teens are subject to significant shifts in mood, even in the same hour, due to hormonal levels.

Teenagers seek to be independent, yet secure in their homes. Life is immediate, dynamic, and, often, emotionally wrenching for them. Any parent will tell you that even the most well-adjusted teen will have his or her trials and tribulations as part of learning to cope in the real world. Even the most mature teenager can be impulsive and narrow in focus.

The suicidal teen has little experience with perspective. Telling him or her that life is not as bad as it seems will be a fruitless exercise. To such a teen, life is not bad—it's *horrible*. To say that he or she should respond in a certain positive way will be equally fruitless. The young person *knows* he or she should be that way, but *can't*. There is a coping problem.

The first task of the counselor, once the teen is out of suicidal danger, is to determine whether there is something else interfering with his or her life—like the use of drugs or alcohol. If there is drug abuse or dependency, no counseling will work unless the addiction is dealt with first. The abuse of drugs, including alcohol, is a significant factor in many teen suicides.

Second, the counselor tries to ascertain what the teen's family life is like. The coping problem or lack of self-esteem may have its root in an abusive family situation that will have to be addressed. Or perhaps there is emotional neglect. Maybe there is no communication. Unless you understand something of the family dynamic, your counseling will not be terribly effective.

After some of this inventory-taking and history-reviewing, you can proceed to deal with the presenting problem: suicide. Have the teen describe what has been driving him or her to the brink. Be sure that you communicate to the teen that you take his or her comments seriously, and that you want to know the story because you care.

Returning to Shneidman's three-fold dynamic of suicide, you will want to get into the person's way of thinking. For example, what is the deep pain in this young person's life? You may encounter a teenage girl who has been sexually abused by her father for some time; she can no longer stand the humiliation and indignity. Not only are you obligated in many states to report this abuse, but you also will have to deal with the girl's confused identity and shame, her fear of men just as she is maturing sexually, and her anger at being abused all those years. This is a deep well of pain, and you would do well to refer such a case to a professional.

Or perhaps you will come across a boy whose girlfriend has just broken up with him. He thinks this is the end of the world, especially if he is an early adolescent. Such a breakup is traumatic for anyone, but the teen has not lived long enough to know that there probably will be other people to love, and who will love him or her. Teen romances are intense and, alas, sexually charged in ways that young people are not yet prepared to handle.

Or perhaps a frightened teenage girl comes to you. She is pregnant. She has very high moral standards, and her parents are active in one of the big churches in town. She cannot "bear to embarrass" them. The girl has convinced herself that the only way out is to kill herself so that she could somehow be a virgin again—and not lose the respect of her parents.

Cases like these are quite common. So are failing to get into the "right" university or college, being fired from a job, being busted for selling drugs, or even failing an important test. All these scenarios involve self-respect, parental love and acceptance, living up to others' expectations as you search to find your own, and coping with making mistakes in judgment. Which of us hasn't had to grapple with issues like these in our own lives? The most honest among us will wonder whether we are all that far ahead of our teenagers in coping.

How might you counsel the three aforementioned teens? You could work to ease their pain in the following ways.

1. With the abused girl, you would want to deal with the pain of being used by another, the pain of being a victim. It would be important to offer a way for the girl to exercise some power in

her terrible circumstances, such as finding a safer place to live.

2. For the boy with the broken romance, you could deal with the pain of rejection by identifying it and relating an experience in which you felt rejected by one you loved.

3. For the pregnant girl, you could begin by helping to name what she feels. Her pain is enveloped in fear and self-loathing. What could you share from your life about being afraid, about hating a mistake you made? She needs to know that she is not alone.

You could also help these three suicidal teens identify their thwarted needs and find ways to meet them as follows.

1. In the abused girl's case, there is a clear example of a thwarted psychological need. How can she possibly feel secure while being abused? How can she know that she is loved when she is used for an adult's sexual kicks—and that adult is her father? You could model a caring relationship which does not threaten. Then you could point out ways in which you asked for her trust and she gave it to you—and you did not abuse it.

2. In the boy's case, there is rejection—a thwarting of his need for acceptance—and a failure of trust. Again, you would want to create an atmosphere of trust. Then you could relate your experiences, pointing out how you are both establishing a relationship that has healthy communication and is free of the pressure to be sexually active.

3. In the pregnant girl's case, the need for self-respect has been thwarted. As a Christian counselor, you would take a clearly non-judgmental approach with this fragile soul, letting her know that, no matter what happens, you will not abandon her because of her pregnancy.

Finally, you could deal with these teens' constriction of options. Your job would be to help provide more options. In each case, you could make a grocery list of all the potential choices the person has—*including* suicide. But you would also emphasize that none of these choices *has* to be acted upon today. Things will wait until tomorrow. You would list in a non-judgmental manner all the options you could think of, then have the person rank the choices in order of preference. The person does not *have to* do any of them. This ranking helps make the matter more objective, less critical. It also forces the person through a logical exercise to confront the twisted logic of suicide in which there is only one choice.

In some of these cases you would want to refer, based on your family assessment. The abused girl would need considerable psychological treatment to undo the damage done to her. The boy would need help from a counselor to see why he was so dependent on his girlfriend that he felt he could not live without her. The pregnant girl might be referred to a Christian pregnancy center which helps unwed mothers make decisions about bringing a baby to term and avoiding abortion.

But you, as a counselor, could intervene to lower the danger level by easing the suffering, meeting some immediate and basic psychological needs, and helping the person think through the crisis.

The Spiritual Side

There is, of course, a spiritual dimension here. I can get at it by telling a story, told to me by another pastor who heads an institution for troubled children.

The institution took in a girl who had been abused by her father for years. She had hardly a shred of self-respect left. As the pastor (who was also a helping professional) worked with her, they made little progress.

Then he said, "You know, you will never get any better unless you can find a way to forgive your father. Otherwise, you will always be bitter."

Her reply was a shriek: "I can never forgive my father for what he's done to me!"

"If you invite Christ into your heart," he said, "you will find the power to forgive."

Session after session went like this. The pastor always concluded with the same remark, in quiet persistence.

One night the girl felt she couldn't take life any more. She made plans to walk to a nearby cliff and jump to a certain death nearly a thousand feet below. As she made her bed and got her jacket, she stopped in her tracks.

The pastor's told me about Christ, she thought, *and I haven't given that a try.* So she said, "Jesus, I don't really believe that You're there, but pastor says You are and that You can help. That's good enough for me. If You really are there, help me know—this is Your chance."

At that moment she felt as if she were being bathed in a warm light and scrubbed inside and out. Finally she fell into a deep and restful sleep.

When she saw the pastor the next morning, she was radiant. "I've never slept so well!" she said. "I did ask Christ into my heart, and I know now that He forgave my father. Now I can."

There was a long way to go, but a long bridge had been crossed because the pastor dared to bring up, quietly and persistently, the girl's spiritual void and her need for healing.

You need to tell the person who has a spiritual void that only Christ can fill it. But the invitation must be absolutely genuine, and part of the overall treatment program (though we know it is a key to the treatment working). This is the kind of counseling that suicidal teens need from Christian counselors and therapists.

Counseling the Elderly

The elderly deal with the reality of death every day. One elderly woman I know had 15 friends die in one year. That's enough to depress even the healthiest person! Elderly people also deal with partial deaths—the decline in the use of the body with aging and illness, increasing isolation, and growing reliance on others. For many, growing old is like becoming a child again. There can be a certain innocence and lack of pretense, but there is also a return to dependence that can be very depressing.

Counseling strategies for suicidal, elderly people, as with teenagers, should use the triad of easing pain, addressing thwarted needs, and opening options. But the counselor must also realize that it is very difficult to change patterns of behavior and coping mechanisms (or lack of them) that elderly persons have lived with for much of their lives. It is possible, but it is hard work. Some helpers have special ministry gifts to deal with this kind of person, who can be particularly needy.

One important part of a counseling strategy is keeping the lines of communication with the outside world as wide open as possible. It's easy for the elderly person to remain isolated in his or her apartment or house, neglected by family (or with family thousands of miles away). As one older woman told me, "When I'm alone too much, I do not think clearly and I get scared." To keep the person socially involved, to maintain regular contact with him or her is crucial, especially after the loss of a loved one. Older people need to know that someone out there cares about them and would like to listen to them as they talk about the past and try to come to grips with the present.

The elderly's need for love and care can easily be thwarted by the sheer absence of people who have time to spend with them. One innovative counseling technique matches a child who needs a little extra attention with an elderly man or woman who needs a "grandchild" close by. It's like the "Dennis the Menace" comic strip, in a way. Mr. Wilson, the irascible, retired neighbor, *needs* Dennis—far more than Dennis needs him. Mr. Wilson may grump about Dennis, but he would find it hard to live without the boy. Pairing a child who needs attention with an elderly person who needs to love and care is a good way to help both.

As life "narrows down," so can an elder's options. Depressed, some older people feel the only choice in a helpless and hopeless life is suicide "so that I won't be a burden on my children." A reality check is very helpful here, as is a kind of historical review. Are there *really* no other options? *Must* suicide be committed *today*? Has that always been true? Then what makes this situation different from those that have come before?

A suicidal elderly person also needs to have a thorough physical exam. Such an exam might turn up reasons for the elder's deep depression. Indeed, much of what passes for senility, dementia, or even the symptoms of Alzheimer's disease can be elements of severe depression that could lead an elderly person to suicide. Proper medication, taken under supervision, can help to restore an elder to the person he or she "really" is.

As the counselor assists the older person in seeking proper medical treatment, the help may become quite practical. Medicare and Medicaid forms need to be completed. Prescriptions need to be filled. The elder may need a ride to the doctor's office. Sometimes home health care has to be arranged.

The counselor need not go it alone in helping the elderly, of course. Today there is a range of options for the care and treatment of older people. The staffs of many mental health centers include specialists in geriatric psychology, and most American communities have programs and services for senior citizens. The object of most of these programs is for people to live the best lives possible outside of institutions. You will find it helpful to discover all you can about the resources available in your area.

The Christian's Special Contribution

The spiritual needs of the elderly are complex, and many issues swirl around death and eternal life. The elder is trying to put his or her entire life into perspective, to make peace before earthly life is done. There is much spiritual counsel to be given an elder who would pray, as David did, "Do not cast me away when I am old; do not forsake me when my strength is gone" (Ps. 71:9). Or, as David prayed later in the psalm, "Even when I am old and gray, do not forsake me, O God, till I declare your power to the next generation, your might to all who are to come" (Ps. 71:18).

The Christian counselor should assure the elder that she or he is not forsaken, that God abides with her or him forever. The elder is not alone, nor forgotten. He or she will not move into oblivion. There is a God who knows each hair on the person's head—even if the hairs are no longer there!

The Christian community can help elderly persons in another way: by visiting them. Some older people require intense psychological counseling, but others' needs are met with supervision of medications, proper nutrition, and a willing ear. That requires time, which many people are unwilling to give. Churches can begin to fill this gap.

One large congregation on whose staff I served had a home visitor for the elderly. Her sole responsibility was the older part of the congregation—which, in that community, was sizable. She looked after various needs of the church's elderly, and took time to hear these men and women tell stories and review their lives. She performed a valuable service. This sort of ministry will become even more important in the near future; in the U.S. the elderly comprise the fastest-growing age group.

In many small churches, and even medium-sized ones, the pastor must visit the elderly. I know what a lot of pastors think about this: *All I need is one more thing on an already crammed schedule!* When I was in that position, I resolved to dedicate one afternoon a week to looking in on shut-ins and elderly persons. I cannot tell you how much I learned from people in those visits. I consider those times some of the best in my ministry. Even half an hour makes all the difference in the world to a housebound elderly person. It sends a message: Somebody cares. That can make life worth living.

The Survivors

A different counseling plan should be followed for those whose loved ones have committed suicide. The focus must be on coming to terms with a profound loss, with the attendant grief process that has already been outlined in the preceding chapter.

To review briefly, Elisabeth Kübler-Ross' five stages of death and dying—which survivors also undergo—are *denial, anger, bargaining, depression,* and *acceptance.* The task of the counselor is to enable survivors to work toward acceptance of the loved one's suicide, and to move on with some measure of grace and well being. As an experienced counselor will testify, this task is not an easy one.

Counseling survivors can be done individually, but sometimes it works well in a group setting, where survivors can hear from others who have "made it" to recovery. Your local mental health office may know of such groups in your area, or you can write the American Association of Suicidology (see the Bibliography) for further information.

The counselor's first task is to gently lead the survivor to the fact that, yes, the person did indeed commit suicide. No, it was not an accident. He or she did mean to do it. This is not some gruesome mistake, and, alas, the family member will not be returning. All this is terribly difficult for a loved one, for it means peering into the pit of death.

Then the counselor will want to pay attention as the person moves into an angry state. The survivor may rage against the loved one: "How could you do this to me?" The person may rage against God: "How could you let this happen?" In the anger, the loved one is trying to make sense out of a senseless, pointless act. The person will even rage against himself or herself. "Could I have been a better mother?" "Could I have been a more caring son?" "Could I have been a better friend?" These are the questions that have no answers, yet they must be asked by the survivor.

Often the person will move into a bargaining position. In this case there's not much to bargain for—except release from pain. By this point the survivor realizes that the loved one cannot be bargained back into existence. But the survivor might pray, "Let me have another chance, Lord, with another person, and I'll do better."

Since there is little for which to bargain, the move into depression is often rather rapid as the person looks inward and comes to grip with the utter sadness of the situation. The survivor may miss the deceased intensely at this point; perhaps a holiday has come and gone without the loved one. Now the body's energy level sinks to a new low. The housework and yard work cannot be done. It is a struggle to get out of bed in the morning. This stage can last for some time, even several months.

Gradually a peace settles in, and the survivor finds some key that helps him or her go on living. Often that key is a renewed relationship with God. As one young widow told me, "I have learned to wake up every morning and to realize that each day is a precious gift from God." This is a level of acceptance at which the survivor can say quietly and matter-of-factly that the loved one has committed suicide. The survivor knows there is nothing to be ashamed of, and there is a part of himself or herself that will always feel empty. But at least the unbearable pain and sadness are gone.

Not everybody makes it through these steps to acceptance, no matter how hard counselors try to help. Some survivors simply never get over the loss; their lives are crippled forever with the memory of the person ever-present in their hearts and minds. One father told me quite sincerely, "I never will understand just what made my son do what he did." The man was obsessed by that thought, and could not find resolution.

Counseling the Presence of God

The suicidal person has two fundamental spiritual problems. First, as the person is swallowed in a vortex of hopelessness, he or she denies the reality of the living God—at least for him or her. God is not present in a way the person can discern. Second, the person's self is at the center of the universe—a failing self, to be sure, but the ego nonetheless. The suicidal person's vision is so narrowed that he or she is utterly unaware of others and their perceptions.

The counselor who seeks to help the suicidal person discover God's presence has a difficult task. But success is made possible by the grace of the living God who intervenes in our lives, in our time. Our culture's forces are arrayed against God; the suicidal person is the most extreme example of self-centeredness, which the culture glorifies.

The truth is that the end of self-centeredness is despair. French existentialist philosopher Jean-Paul Sartre found that self-absorption evoked in him a feeling of nausea. Not very pleasant—except that Sartre rejoiced. At least he could feel *something* besides emptiness!

Suicide attempters and completers no longer can stand themselves or their existence. As Seward Hiltner wrote in his seminal work, *Pastoral Counseling* (Abingdon Press, 1969): "People get sick emotionally not only because of immediate frustrations but also because they are troubled about their own meaning and destiny." The suicidal person is gripped at a fundamental level by this problem.

If I cannot stand myself as I am; if I am an utter failure; if I am totally helpless to change my situation because I have no power; if I am totally alone, forsaken by all, then I have only one alternative. I must kill myself. In my annihilation, I will be nothing. That's better than being less than nothing in this life.

This is the spiritual problem. What shall we say to the person who sees life in this way?

We must affirm again and again, "God is *for* you. He is not against you. He is *with* you, and will never leave you." As counselors, we will have to embody this truth. We will have to mediate this truth of God by the power of the Holy Spirit. Otherwise, these are just so many empty words. The suicidal person desperately wants to believe these words, but has no context in which to evaluate them.

There is Scripture on which we can pattern our affirmation of God's presence. But we must integrate this teaching into our counseling, not quote a string of proof texts as if the suicidal person cån accept them at face value. We have to work inductively. Israel's experience as recorded in the Old Testament is a wonderful counseling tool. Let's look at just three examples.

1. *Isaiah*. This prophet spoke words of hope even as the kingdom was falling to pieces and the Exile was taking place. The people had believed they were utterly forsaken and forgotten by God. What a sense of despair!

To them, and to their situation, the Lord spoke through the prophet Isaiah: "Shout for joy, O heavens; rejoice, O earth; burst into song, O mountains! For the Lord comforts his people, and will have compassion on his afflicted ones.

"But Zion said, 'The Lord has forsaken me, the Lord has forgotten me.'

"Can a mother forget the baby at her breast and have no compassion on the child she has borne? Though she may forget, I will not forget you! See, I have engraved you on the palms of

65

my hands; your walls are ever before me" (Isa. 49:13-16).

This is our starting point in spiritual counsel and direction with those who have attempted suicide. We can say to the suicidal person, "You've said you feel abandoned and worthless. But others have felt like you—entire peoples have felt like you. That's part of being human, the problem of being human. Yet God did not forget His people, and never forgets them. He has not forgotten you. And I want to model this for you."

2. *Hosea.* The prophet Hosea also speaks to this point. He modeled in his marriage what was happening to the people of Israel. Hosea was a faithful husband, but his wife was unfaithful. Indeed, she became a prostitute. She repented and returned, though she felt completely worthless. Hosea accepted her with joy, but warned that she should not stray again. This is like the Lord, who would accept the people. "I will show my love to the one I called 'Not my loved one.' I will say to those called 'Not my people', 'You are my people'; and they will say, 'You are my God'" (Hos. 2:23).

3. *David.* As already suggested, the Psalms are a fruitful place for spiritual counsel. I have often found Psalm 22 helpful. The suicidal person can almost always identify with David, who cries out his feeling of forsakenness. Yet if you read this psalm carefully, you will see hope as well. On the one hand, David expresses his despair; on the other he remembers the truth of God. He feels forsaken; yet he recognizes that God is almighty, enthroned upon the cherubim, and that God has been with him since before he was born. In this anguish of the soul, David finally takes on trust that God will be there for him, and that God is worthy to be praised on that account alone.

So we learn from the Old Testament to counsel the presence of God by *remembrance*. God remembers us; indeed, he knows us each by name, and knew us while we were yet in the womb. When we despair, we need to remember God's remembrance of us. We can claim God's promise never to forget or forsake us.

At some point the suicidal person may begin to see that he or she has been doubting God's promise to care for him or her. Indeed, the person may have doubted or denied the very existence of a caring, loving God. As he or she reaches this point in healing it is appropriate for repentance to take place. Remember that repentance is the intent to live a new way, God's way, and to leave behind a former way of life—to die to self so that we can be reborn. To the suicidal person, this may be a great relief—the chance to start over again.

Counseling the presence of God from the New Testament focuses on *resurrection*. This point will apply more and more as the suicidal person moves away from the crisis. You will not want to talk about death and resurrection while the person is in danger of taking his or her own life, but as his or her commitment to live grows more secure you can help by reflecting on the subject.

In the Gospel according to John, Jesus raises His friend Lazarus from the dead. But before that, Jesus assures Lazarus' sister Martha that her brother will rise again. She quotes some wonderful theology about rising on the last day. Jesus replies that He is the resurrection and the life, and that those who believe in Him shall live, even though they die physically (John 11:25, 26).

Jesus Himself is the source of life for all people who believe in Him, though they die. This is what suicidal people have experienced—a kind of death, though not a physical one. They have died to all that this world has to offer, because they know that the world offers only pablum and nothing of real or lasting substance.

Jesus can be the source of life because He has been raised from the dead. On the cross He bore all our sin, guilt, wickedness, hopelessness, and despair. He summed it all up in His cry from Psalm 22:1: "My God, my God, why have you forsaken me?" (Matt. 27:46)

In being raised from the dead, Jesus has crushed the power of sin and death. He is the only hope for those who grapple with their utter sinfulness and their wish to die, the clearest evidence we have that sin and death do not have the last word. We need to counsel the presence of God in resurrection, and offer resurrection life to those in despair.

The Challenge of Counseling

"The people walking in darkness have seen a great light; on those living in the land of the shadow of death a light has dawned" (Isa. 9:2). This is good news that the Christian counselor can bring to the suicidal person. But bringing this message can be very hard work, made possible by the living grace of the living God.

The suicidal person must be rebuilt from the inside out. This is a great work of God, but it is also a responsibility laid upon us as counselors. We had better know from the beginning that fulfilling our charge won't be easy. It will take much prayer on our part to be fortified to serve.

The suicidal person has been to such depths. He has stared into the pit; she has confronted the awful reality of life without God. The journey back is a long one. My pastor friend, whose story I recounted earlier, worked long and hard to earn the trust of the suicidal girl before he could introduce her to the living Lord. Even then there was no assurance that she would turn to Christ. The important thing was that my friend did not stand in judgment over her; he accepted her as she was, with all her pain, weakness, and limitations. He let the Spirit of God work in her and prayed for her regularly.

That is a good example for those of us who choose the difficult yet exciting task of counseling those who are face the crisis of suicide.

CHAPTER FIVE

SPREADING THE WORD IN YOUR CHURCH

I F YOU WANT TO HELP THE SUICIDAL, YOU'LL ALSO WANT TO help others to become aware of the problem of suicide, some of the dynamics involved, and how to be a friend to one who faces this crisis.

Our tendency is to flee from a person in such great psychological pain, for he or she reminds us of our own frailty and mortality. To overcome this problem in Christian circles, a lot of teaching needs to be done about the nature of true friendship. The suicidal person really needs more friends to listen, and fewer friends to give pep talks and advice.

This chapter features a curriculum outline designed to raise awareness in your church concerning suicide and what people can do to help. Christian education is a key to helping lower the rate of suicide, to equip members of the body to minister intelligently and compassionately.

Learning more about suicide can enable many in a congregation to spot a potentially suicidal person, and to intervene where appropriate. Only those with specific psychological training should treat the suicidal person, but anyone can help to prevent suicide or care for a person who is on the road to recovery.

These curriculum outlines can be modified to suit any congregation. The topics are excellent ones for a community association of churches or two or three denominational congregations to address together. In doing so, you could minister widely in your community and cooperate to see lives saved.

Before presenting these sessions, you might want to discover whether suicide is a present concern to your congregation. You could ask the question this way, perhaps in a Sunday service, to be answered in writing: "How many of you know someone, closely or distantly, who has attempted suicide?" Then, "How many in the last two years?" Then, "Have you ever thought about taking your own life at any time?"

You will want to assure absolute confidentiality in this

exercise, of course—so don't ask for names. You might even give everyone the same kind of pencil. You may be surprised at the results. People are more familiar with suicide than we might think. Because it is familiar and affects people's lives so deeply, there may be heightened interest even without some kind of community crisis to precipitate it.

A Short Course in Suicide Prevention

This curriculum can be taught in four one-hour sessions. Participants should expect to attend the four sessions, take part in discussion, and, by the end of the class, be able to identify potentially suicidal behavior so they can intervene and lead the suicidal person to help.

The class leader should be a trained Christian counselor. He or she will find it helpful to refer to other chapters in this book.

SESSION 1: THE FACTS ABOUT SUICIDE

1. Outline what the four-week program is designed to accomplish.

2. Discuss suicide from a statistical viewpoint. How likely is it that someone will commit suicide?

A. American statistics for incidence in the population.

B. Statistics broken down by age, sex, and racial group.

1. Emphasize that the elderly male is most at risk.

2. Note that suicide is the eighth leading cause of death in the U.S., and third leading for teens (and on the rise in that group).

C. Break down statistics into "bite-sized" chunks: numbers per minute who attempt, per day who succeed.

D. If obtainable, get statistics for your metropolitan area or county.

3. Put a human face on the statistics.

A. Ask participants whether they can recall any famous people who committed suicide; be prepared to name a few (Marilyn Monroe always gets a mention).

B. Ask participants to break into small groups to

answer the question, "Who do I know who has attempted suicide, or been successful?" This will be a way for participants to get to know one another. Groups should contain six to eight people. When responding to the question, participants should be encouraged to tell something about the individual and the circumstances of the suicide. As full a tale as is comfortable can be told.

4. Some common threads of suicides.

A. Ask group members to report on what they learned from the stories, what common threads and differences they noticed.

B. List those common points (notes, absence of notes, life situations, previous attempts, etc.)

C. Suggest that these points will be mentioned in greater detail next session, which will deal with traits of the suicidal person.

SESSION 2: TRAITS OF THE SUICIDAL

1. Note that last week participants began to identify traits or patterns of the suicidal person, and that this week you will study them in greater depth.

2. Explain that suicide is an extreme solution to a breakdown somewhere in a person's life; the solution has its own twisted logic to it, as well as involving deep feeling.

A. The person has an unbearable level of psychological pain.

B. There is a thwarted psychological need, such as security, trust, self-esteem, dignity, etc.

C. There is a narrowing of perceived options to only one: suicide.

D. There is a fundamental lack of coping skills in the person's life.

E. Some personal crisis has precipitated the urge to commit suicide.

F. There is a huge spiritual void in the person, too, which prevents her or him from finding hope in her or his circumstances.

3. List societal and cultural factors influencing suicide.

A. Men in particular are supposed to be productive and competitive; when they retire or become disabled as they age, they lose their guiding values.

B. Increasing mobility makes it hard to establish lasting friendships that can help one feel connected to others.

C. The family unit is very fragile—cite the number of single-parent families and the number of children in them; there is little stability in the family unit.

D. There often is little communication in the family that would allow problems to be shared and solved.

E. Among young people, there is an ethic of instant gratification and pleasure; pain and trial are something to avoid.

F. There is an increasing level of violence on television, in rock song lyrics, and as part of the background of society, including the ever-present threat of nuclear annihilation.

4. Discuss listening to the suicidal person. How can you tell if the person might be suicidal?

A. Read one of the case studies in this book.

B. Break into small groups to answer the question: "Having learned about the traits of the suicidal person, what traits can you identify in the case study? What could you have noticed if you had been a loved one of this individual?"

C. After the large group has reassembled, have people report their reflections. Was the assignment easy or hard? Why?

D. Stress that, with careful listening, it is possible to pick up the signals that a suicidal person is sending out, like an SOS—sometimes a strong signal, sometimes faint.

E. Note that next week you will be dealing with the responsibilities one has as a friend of a suicidal person.

SESSION 3: THROUGH THE VALLEY OF THE SHADOW
1. Review the traits of the suicidal person. Note that

we are responsible to act in friendship toward the suicidal person, and that in this session you'll talk about some tools that can help you to be a better friend.

A. Explain that, while legal matters will be covered in Session 4, you must emphasize now that each of us has a responsibility to help a person who has indicated that he or she intends to commit suicide.

B. Stress also the need for psychological help in a suicidal person's situation; participants should not try to be amateur psychologists.

2. What are some signs that a person is walking through the valley of the shadow of death where suicide is concerned?

A. An outright threat.

1. Ask for details on how he/she plans to accomplish the act—the more specific, the more likely.

B. Previous attempts, if any; if recent, the probability is high.

C. Clear behavioral change from well-adjusted to depressed; active to lethargic; or from depressed to cheerful in a very short period of time.

D. Falling grades or failing performance at work.

E. Drug or alcohol abuse.

F. Anxiety, violent outbursts, relationships in trouble.

3. Intervention strategies.

A. Emergency: Call the police.

B. Urgent, but not critical: Determine whether the person is receiving professional help; if so, call the counselor or psychiatrist. If not, refer that person to a professional—a pastoral counselor, member of the clergy, a psychologist known to you, etc.

C. Check on the person regularly to see whether he or she is all right.

D. Be a helping friend as you realize some of the contributing factors to suicidal behavior.

1. Do what you can to ease the pain; listen; share with the person your own struggles.

2. Try to provide for the thwarted need as carefully as you can by being someone who can be trusted, who cares, who is steadfast.

 3. Help outline some other options the person has to broaden narrow thinking—though avoid pep talks about a silver lining behind every cloud.

 4. Pray for the person regularly, and with the person as you deem appropriate.

 5. Remind the person that he or she is loved by God and is a child of God, and that God is always remembering him or her.

4. Some Biblical insights in walking through the valley of the shadow of death.

 A. God's *remembrance*, with particular focus on Isaiah 49:16; Psalm 22; 23. God knows each of us by name and holds us in the palm of His hand.

 B. Jesus' *resurrection*, which frees us from the power of sin and death and gives us the power to be reborn and remade. There is hope!

5. Close the session by reading the poem "Footsteps" (available on greeting card or plaque in many Christian bookstores).

SESSION 4: MORAL, LEGAL, AND MEDICAL DIMENSIONS
1. Explain that there are certain legal and moral responsibilities we have to help the suicidal person. We should also be aware of the possible organic influence on suicidal behavior. Finally, we must resolve personally to intervene in favor of life.

2. Discuss suicide and the law as follows.

 A. Suicide formerly was a felony in many states, now only in a few. It is usually seen as temporary insanity, with the person unable to help himself or herself.

 B. In most states, someone who becomes aware of a suicidal person is required to intervene [check your own state's laws]. That intervention generally means referring the person to professional help or asking the police to become involved in a situation of imminent danger.

 C. Cases ruled suicide by coroners are probably fewer than those that actually occur, since insurance death benefits do not pay for suicidal death.

 D. The state realizes the individual's freedom is

tempered by the common good; suicide would harm the common good, or so the law believes.

3. Outline moral duties—we are our brother's keeper.

A. Review the story of the Good Samaritan (Luke 10:25-37).

B. Point out that we are the Body of Christ (I Cor. 12) and members of one another in that Body.

4. Explain medical dimensions.

A. Suicide, as it is linked with depression, may have organic, or physiological, causes—it is not only self-centered despair.

B. Possible hereditary links are being explored.

5. Review resources in your community for referral.

A. Could participants volunteer for a helpline such as that run by the Samaritans?

B. Should your church start a counseling program?

C. What will students do with this learning?

6. Close with the hymn, "How Firm a Foundation," and with prayer for those in danger of suicide.

These outlines can be adapted in any way which helps the learning process. The small group activities at the beginning could be important to establish group cohesiveness, and to put the learning to work more directly.

There should be some action step at the end, the nature of which may become evident as the group meets. How is God calling you and your congregation to respond to the increase in suicides, particularly among teens?

You may want to obtain from your local mental health society some literature on suicide and depression, so that participants can refer to it outside and after the sessions.

A Support Group for Survivors

You may also want to consider starting a support group for those whose loved ones have committed suicide. Many cities and towns do not have groups like this. Yet survivors need to find others who share the same awful experience—that they may feel less alone.

How would such a meeting be structured?

The counselor would act as a consultant for the group. He or she would not actually lead the meeting; this would be done by a survivor who is relatively far along in resolving his or her own relative's suicide. The leader could also request the counselor's suggestions and observations outside the weekly meeting. The leader would do well to realize that the membership of the group would change regularly, with people coming and going.

The group's model could be the Twelve Step Program popularized by Alcoholics Anonymous. Developed for alcoholics in recovery, it is a pattern many other recovery groups follow. Over the years it has been remarkably effective in helping people begin to manage their lives and their difficulties, to find serenity, and to begin recovery.

The Twelve Step Program puts responsibility for recovery in the person's own hands. At the same time it recognizes that a person is powerless to recover from his or her condition without the help of God. So the program is God-centered, not human-centered. Finally, the program recognizes human limitations. There are times when a person fails at recovery, when he or she falls back into old habits. Recovery is never complete in this life; it is always a process. Thus the program is open-ended, with people working at their own pace.

Here are adapted versions of the Twelve Steps, based on those found in *Alcoholics Anonymous* (Alcoholics Anonymous World Services Inc., 1976). They could help survivors to deal with grief and, where needed, to improve family relationships that may have contributed to the suicide.

1. We admit we are powerless to recover by ourselves.

2. We believe that a Power greater than ourselves can restore us.

3. We decide to turn over our wills and lives to God's care.

4. We make a searching, fearless moral inventory of ourselves.

5. We admit to God, to ourselves, and to another human being the exact nature of our wrongs.

6. We are ready to have God remove all these defects of character.

7. We humbly ask Him to remove our shortcomings.

8. We make a list of persons we have harmed, and become willing to make amends to them all.

9. We make direct amends to such people wherever possible, except when doing so would injure them or others.

10. We take personal inventory, and when we are wrong we promptly admit it.

11. We seek through prayer and meditation to improve our conscious contact with God, praying for knowledge of His will for us and the power to carry that out.

12. Having had a spiritual awakening as a result of these steps, we try to carry this message to others who suffer and to practice these principles in all our affairs.

Such a group should also discuss patterns of grief, such as those stated by Elisabeth Kübler-Ross and cited elsewhere in this book. The group should provide an environment in which people can openly share their feelings—which may be very intense at times—but it also must include content that people can absorb at an intellectual level.

Here is a meeting outline, plus tips on facilitating an effective group.

Survivors' Meeting
1. Welcome (10 minutes)
The group leader welcomes everyone to the meeting, especially those who are present for the first time. The leader introduces himself or herself, then asks the rest to give their names. Then the leader explains the purpose of the meeting by reading or saying some-

thing like the following:

"We have come together because we share a common experience. Someone we love has committed suicide. We also share in the struggle to find peace so that we may move on with our lives and not be trapped forever by this overwhelming loss.

"We are a fellowship of survivors. Each of us has dignity as a human being in the presence of God. We must listen to one another with respect and compassion. We must also respect those who do not wish to talk, but would rather listen, reflect, and pray. Most importantly, we must respect the confidentiality of what is shared here so that the bonds of this fellowship may grow stronger.

"We are seeking healing from our sadness and pain. But we also are seeking understanding and knowledge so that we can find healing in our minds. Our aim is to be informed so that we can help others in need and intervene when necessary so that this tragedy does not happen to another whom we know and love.

"We recognize the need for divine power to aid in our healing and our understanding. Many of us know the power of prayer to heal and transform broken lives. There will be people available to pray with you, if you desire, after the end of the meeting."

2. Sharing Time (20-30 minutes)

The leader begins this section by giving his or her name again, along with brief summaries of the following: personal experience with suicide; how he or she is feeling tonight; personal progress on the Twelve Step Program; new insights he or she might have gained during the week.

In this way the example is set for others to share, or to "pass" if they do not wish to participate by speaking (though they will participate as they listen).

3. Learning Time (20-30 minutes)

The leader might review the stages of grief, explain one of the Twelve Steps, share something about the psychology of suicide or recovery, or present other material relevant to the group's purpose. It is important that the material be clear to first-timers as well as helpful to those who are further along. Time for questions and answers should be provided.

4. Reflection Time (10 minutes)

At this time people may be quiet, pray, read, or simply sit and do nothing. It is important to include this time for thinking about everything that has been said—and unsaid—during the meeting.

5. Closing Prayer

Keep it brief—perhaps something like this from the Episcopal *Book of Common Prayer:* "Almighty God, Father of mercies and giver of comfort: Deal graciously, we pray, with all who mourn; that, casting all their care on you, they may know the consolation of your love; through Jesus Christ our Lord. Amen."

6. Fellowship Time

Those who wish may stay for coffee and cookies, look over a literature table, or go into another room to pray for healing for themselves and others.

Some Tips

Keep the meeting moving along without rushing people in their sharing. It's easy for someone to dominate unless an active leader focuses comments and encourages others to contribute.

The learning section could be led by a professional counselor who has an ongoing relationship with the group. A pastor may be called on from time to time to raise spiritual issues. Don't turn the group into a Bible study, however, and don't force your point of view on the participants. Remember that group members are very vulnerable at the meeting.

Provide suitable literature for people to take with them. The Stephen Ministries and the American Association of Suicidology have tracts and leaflets. Other material on such subjects as prayer, the spiritual life, and healing may be purchased from Christian publishing houses. Participants should be expected to contribute to cover the cost of these materials.

No fee should be charged for the group, though an offering basket could be placed on a table to allow members to help pay for the room, coffee and supplies, and other incidentals.

Each quarter, send out publicity on the group meeting to area places of worship, psychologists and therapists, pastoral counseling agencies, mental health clinics, and hospitals. Make your meetings known through your local newspaper, too.

From time to time you may wish to bring in a special speaker to supplement—not replace—the weekly meeting. This can be a strong boost to group members.

As the group develops a history, leadership can be passed around to a variety of people. Alcoholics Anonymous groups call it "sharing the lead." The counselor can help assess the readiness of particular individuals to lead.

Finally, please use first names only. You want to address one another personally, and many participants may know each other, but it is also important to maintain anonymity. Group members should be cautioned not to talk about anyone's contributions to the discussion, or even membership in the meeting, unless that person has granted permission.

A Balanced Approach

A good curriculum dealing with suicide prevention or suicide survivors needs to view content as both intellectual and emotional. That is true for any effective learning model, but all the more so with suicide—since the very act strikes so profoundly at basic life issues.

To teach or lead groups to discuss suicide offers a wonderful and subtle way to talk theologically about God's desire for human life. The Bible is a superb textbook, not only on God's loving sovereignty, but also on sinful—and redeemed—human nature.

The questions, "Why would anyone want to commit suicide?" and "Why shouldn't anyone commit suicide?" find response in God's Word. That Word can help us interpret the secular and scientific theories on suicide—which we will seek to do in the next chapter.

CHAPTER SIX

THEORY AND THEOLOGY

S UICIDE HAS BEEN PART OF HUMAN LIFE FROM NEARLY THE dawn of history. It is known in every culture, though different cultures deal with it in different ways.

The ancient Greeks saw suicide as a noble act of free choice when convicted of a crime. The philosopher Socrates, for example, drank poisonous hemlock upon his conviction rather than suffer the humiliation of being put to death by the authorities.

In traditional Japanese culture, vanquished soldiers would rather have committed *hara-kiri* than be slaves to a foreign power. In World War II, kamikaze pilots willingly flew their planes into American ships, guaranteeing death for themselves and hoping for glory for their country and cause.

In India, among certain castes, widows throw themselves upon the burning funeral pyres of their dead husbands. This practice has been outlawed in modern India, but has not disappeared completely.

In Western culture a different view of suicide developed. Today this view continues to shape our theological and legal understanding of the person and the act.

The Church and Suicide

The Catholic Church stated its early opposition to suicide, placing suicide in the same category as murder—murder of self. The Church affirmed the sanctity of all human life as the creation of God. Any willful taking of life was deemed an affront to God, and a sin of the most heinous sort. In the eyes of the Church, the suicidal person was committed to hell for denying the very gift of God, life itself.

The sanctity of life as a theological position was refined during the medieval period. In an age when death was so near to families, and life was clearly understood to be fragile, the very thought of taking one's own life was a fundamental absurdity.

In Europe, legal systems emerged from the Church's institutional structure. In old English law, one who clearly had committed suicide was denied a burial plot in the town, and the Church forbade a Christian burial. The corpse was tied to the back of a horse and pulled through the streets to the town crossroads, a symbolic spot and a reminder to passersby of the indignity and shamefulness of this death. The corpse was thrown into a crude grave and hastily covered up. The family was subject to the confiscation of property from the deceased's estate, since he was considered a felon.

The conviction of suicide, however, was rarely applied—because the English legal tradition, which Americans inherited, presumed innocence until guilt could be proved beyond a reasonable doubt. A person would not commit suicide, the argument went, because the impulse goes against his or her drive to live and to preserve life. So suicide convictions were few and far between.

The Church—Catholic, Protestant, and Reformed—still upholds the sanctity of life as a fundamental theological position. Up to this century, Christian burial would be denied a suicide victim in many congregations, and the family would have been shunned because of the criminal nature of the act. There was a sense of taboo surrounding suicide, a desire not even to acknowledge its occurrence.

Today the Church's fundamental assertion that life is sacred must be supplemented—by the assertion that God is lovingly present in a future that is temporally uncertain but under His sovereign authority. That is, we don't know what the future holds, but we cling to the promises of God to be with us to the end. We know that He never abandons nor forsakes us. That is the ground for hope. God created life; He sustains it today; He will bring it to fruition and completion in His time. And He makes life eternal available through Jesus Christ.

We make these assertions because Western society is losing sight of the meaning and purpose of human life. The West of the late 20th century has repeatedly challenged the sanctity of life. Now the suicidal person is the symbol of Western despair, of existential anxiety in a world seemingly without God. He or she is a symptom of a deeper illness in our culture and society.

This despairing philosophy is summed up in the song made popular in the 1960s by singer Peggy Lee: "Is That All There Is?" We recognize this hopelessness in our music, movies, and novels, all reflections of our culture. The Church must contend with these cultural realities as it seeks to minister to the troubled, hopeless, and confused.

Psychological Theories and Suicide

Today the Church's teaching on suicide has changed, not in its basic assertions, but in pastoral practice. That practice has been informed by psychology.

The father of psychoanalysis, Sigmund Freud, was a student of suicide. He observed suicidal tendencies in nearly all his patients, and began to develop theories about the cause.

In his early work Freud articulated the "pleasure principle." That is, humans instinctively seek out pleasure and avoid pain and suffering. If one enjoys pain and suffering, he or she is in some way sick. Freud called the life-affirming force Eros, and said it drives men and women to love and sexual relationships. His view of human nature on this score was positive.

But Freud also recognized that human beings seek to harm themselves and others. At first he saw this as evidence of displaced hostility toward an unobtainable object of love. But his reflections grew more sober after the haunting experience of a world war. Freud then devised the theory of the death instinct, which he called Thanatos. Human beings were a battleground between Eros and Thanatos.

Thanatos worked in a person's psyche to bring the superego—the accusing parent figure—to awareness. The ego was threatened by this superego. It was as if I, an adult, did something I knew to be wrong—and my hostile mother or father appeared and said as if I were three or four years old, "Bad boy! Don't ever do that again! What a fool!"

Some individuals cannot cope with this critical voice. They do not have enough ego strength. Slowly but surely, they are swallowed by Thanatos.

Freud's theory is complex. Yet anyone who has worked with the suicidal can relate stories of those who felt absolutely driven to attempt suicide. To Freud, the only recourse from suicide was intense psychoanalytic work so that one could find enough love and hope to live.

Freud's early students, Alfred Adler and William Stekel, developed their own theories on suicide. Adler suggested that suicide was the result of an inferiority complex, a desire for revenge on one who has been hurtful, or an antisocial regression into a more primitive form of coping. Stekel linked suicide to masturbation and attendant feelings of guilt. There may be some elements of truth here, particularly in Adler's thinking. But Freud's work remains the foundation for a psychoanalytic approach to suicide.

In 1897 sociologist Emile Durkheim published a seminal and brilliant work, *The Sociology of Suicide*, in which he considered cultural factors as well as individual psychological traits that might lead a person to suicide. He proposed three types of suicides: egoistic, altruistic, and anomic.

The egoistic suicide is committed by a person who has been inadequately socialized into a group and its structure. The altruistic suicide is one in which a person kills himself or herself out of duty and honor for society; he or she might also be called a martyr in some circles. The anomic suicide stems from a lack of societal restraint on individual passions; the person can no longer cope. This kind of suicide has become more frequent in Western culture.

Durkheim's work may not help us spot a potential suicide nor learn how to intervene effectively. But his framework enables us to understand why psychological interest in the subject has grown. Not only are we recognizing more deaths as suicides, but there are simply more of them—and our culture increasingly, but very subtly, encourages self-destruction.

There are limitations, however, to Durkheim's theory. As critic A. Alvarez wrote in his book on suicide, *The Savage God* (Random House, 1972), "The broad effect of Durkheim's masterpiece was to insist that suicide was not an irredeemable moral crime but a fact of society, like the birth rate or the rate of productivity; it had social causes which were subject to discernable laws and could be discussed or analyzed rationally." Alvarez notes that social engineering will not change human nature. Even if we did understand the social sources of suicide, the mystery of the person who decides to take his own life would remain.

Meanwhile, Freud's students have refined their mentor's thinking on suicide. Karl Menninger, for example, suggests that there are three components of suicide in the individual: the wish to kill, the wish to be killed, and the wish to die. This is a complex interaction within a person's psyche. One who tries to commit suicide may want to kill only part of himself or herself so that life can be bearable. The problem is, of course, that to annihilate part of ourselves we must kill all of ourselves. We are not modular units which can be added or discarded at will.

Another psychologist, Maurice Farber of the University of Connecticut, offers further analysis of suicide which combines individual and societal influences. He writes of "the situational factor" in his book, *Theory of Suicide* (Arno Press, 1977).

The situational factor, Farber says, is "the degree of threat leveled against the individual's being able to sustain a minimally acceptable existence." The personal part of this formula is competence—the person's sense of having the resources to cope with life's demands. This sense is instilled—or should be—when a person is very young.

But society helps to provide the context for competence. Like individuals, societies despair and hope. So a given person's potential to be suicidal depends on his or her inner resources for coping, and the outer resources of hoping. Does the person have a sense of worth and competence, or has that been damaged in early life? What are the demands on his or her coping skills? Is the person in relationships that give as well as take? Does society see suicide as an acceptable "solution," or at least a neutral one?

Farber reminds us that we are social beings, not just individual atoms making free, rational choices. We are accountable to each other for our personal decisions. We participate in a greater trend of hope or despair in our culture—and the prevailing attitude in our culture tends to be boredom bordering on hopelessness.

Suicide: Today's Way Out?

Edwin Shneidman, the psychologist already referred to in this book, says that "suicide is the desperate act of a perturbed and constricted mind, in seemingly unbearable and unresolvable pain. That pain is driven by blocked or unfulfilled psychological needs, which the suicidal person feels are critical for psychological survival."

These needs can be very deep and long-standing. If they cannot be met, then there must be escape. "In this state, people view annihilation, cessation, escape to a better universe, or loss of life as a more attractive option than the torment of life with these needs unmet."

85

Unfortunately, our society has confused needs with wants, raising our expectations of what should rightfully be ours. We have become a narcissistic culture, concerned with self-fulfillment and self-realization. Even as we acquire more material things, we find a void at the center where real needs are—the need to love and be loved, to contribute to life in some meaningful way, to trust in another's love and care and commitment, and to be secure.

In our narcissism we resist committing ourselves to anything that does not promise to quickly comfort us or help us. We do not pursue goals that are big enough to draw us beyond ourselves. We rebel against authority, against anything that could keep us from getting our own way. We especially rebel against religious authority and the idea of God's sovereignty.

The result? As Alvarez sums up, "When neither high purpose nor the categorical imperatives of religion will do, the only argument against suicide is life itself." And that argument is fragile, indeed, because life itself is so fragile.

Even the most well-adjusted life has peaks and valleys. All of us have felt as David did when he wrote, "Oh, that I had the wings of a dove! I would fly away and be at rest—I would flee far away and stay in the desert; I would hurry to my place of shelter, far from the tempest and storm" (Ps. 55:6-8). The Christian can testify that God is with us in trouble—yet we are asked by Jesus to deny ourselves, take up our crosses, and follow Him.

This is unpopular in our age, when we have come to expect life to be easy, comfortable, and generous. Many of us, running up against the hardness of being human, cannot cope. That is why psychologist M. Scott Peck wrote three important words at the beginning of his book, *The Road Less Traveled* (Simon and Schuster, 1980): "Life is difficult."

Our problem may be that we too easily confuse the difficult and the unbearable. So the argument against suicide—life itself—is inherently unsatisfactory. The question, "Why commit suicide?" is easily dismissed in selfishness, hedonistic affluence, and boredom with another question: "Why not?"

Quality of Life vs. Sanctity of Life

"Why not?" is also a question raised by those who emphasize quality of life over sanctity of life. If you no longer feel life is worth living, they say, you should have the freedom to choose death. Most advocates of this view stress that there must be certain compelling factors by which to judge the worth of your own life. But they also hold that personal freedom to judge and choose outweigh any external authority's right to limit choice for the "common good."

The quality of life argument is advanced, for example, by Doris Portwood in her book, *Commonsense Suicide: The Final Right* (Hemlock Society, 1983). Portwood is concerned about the elderly, whom she correctly notes have the highest incidence of suicide among all age groups. She says that, from the point of view of elderly people she has known, suicide makes sense. They have contributed to life, but in many cases are now ashamed to live in dependency and poverty. Chronic illness besets them, causing untold suffering— not to mention the tremendous financial cost that our elders believe drains resources that could be better used elsewhere. Portwood contends that if elderly people feel their lives no longer have the quality of being human, and if they feel intense suffering, it is inhuman to deny them the right to decide what to do with their lives.

According to Portwood, suicide remains "a sin, a crime, and a shame" thanks to the restraining forces of church and state. It is time, she says, to undo those restraints for the sake of personal freedom.

Portwood emphasizes that she advocates this right to choose for the elderly—a line of thought related to arguments for euthanasia, or so-called mercy-death or mercy-killing in situations of extreme illness. Other voices in our society, however, would not limit this right to choose to the elderly. They would extend it to all people.

In a provocative article in the *Southwestern Law Journal* (volume 36, number 4), for example, Michele Malloy and H. Tristram Englehardt, Jr., a lawyer and a doctor, argue that sanctions against suicide and assisting suicide should be removed. Their case is based first on the assertion that individuals should not be coerced by a force outside themselves:

> The very nature of moral uncertainty in pluralist
> secular societies shifts the core of the general
> fabric of morality to respect for the rights of the

individuals to pursue their vision of the good life with consenting others. The focus is then upon protecting the unwilling from coercion and providing refuseable welfare rights, rather than supporting a particular view of the good life through governmental regulation.

The authors say we should support a basic societal concept articulated by Supreme Court Justice Brandeis in 1928—the right to be left alone over against the paternalistic interests of the state. People may not always choose wisely, but the individual's right to choose must prevail over the state's force of coercion. The authors state further, "Although one may not be able to agree about what constitutes good life, or good death, one can agree to let each make his own choices, as long as those choices do not involve direct and significant violence against others."

Let us note two guiding assumptions in this argument. First, the state is the creation of free individuals, not the creator of individual rights and freedoms. A person has the inherent right to do as he or she pleases, without interference, unless violence is done to others. The state has no inherent rights. This challenges the Anglo-American assumption that there can be an offense against the state—one rationale for legal sanctions against suicide and assisting another in the act.

Second, human society is based, not on force, but on reason and peaceful manipulation. People are reasonable; we should trust in their ability to make rational choices that are good for them, as long as they do not directly harm another.

The first assumption has been popularly translated, "Do your own thing." Or, "My values are good for me if I've chosen them, and yours are good for you. Don't impose your values on someone else; that does violence to the person's freedom and dignity." You can see how this would challenge the notion of suicide intervention. This idea will be further addressed in Chapter 7.

The second assumption is more crucial to the psychological and spiritual dimensions of suicide. It is that human beings are inherently rational and will make choices that are good for them—whether choosing a good life or a good death. This argument seems to come from the easy chair, from parlor conversation by the fire after a nice dinner; it is thoroughly out of touch with real life.

Suicide does have the appearance of a rational choice. But the suicidal person does not simply add up the reasons for living in Column A, and the reasons for killing himself or herself in Column B, and find Column A wanting. He or she operates from a fundamentally distorted view of the world—not only his or her world, but *the* world of other persons, of prevailing culture, of God's sovereignty.

Psychologist Edwin Shneidman notes the terrible logic of suicide; it seems to be the only logical solution at the time. Irving Berent summed this up in the provocative title of his book, *The Algebra of Suicide* (Human Science Press, 1981). As one despairing person told me: "One and one just don't add up to two anymore. I'm not sure they ever did in my life."

Indeed, the suicidal are obsessed with the logic of their death, even the logic of their act. Jerry Johnston, in his book, *Why Suicide?* (Thomas Nelson Publishers, 1987) tells the story of Jay, a teen who killed himself. It is clear that Jay had carefully planned how his body would be discovered, how the event should be interpreted, and how his funeral should be handled.

Was Jay's act logical? Psychologists suggest that suicide is a logical act based on a fundamentally irrational perception of the world. They also observe that there is tremendous ambivalence in suicide; the person is saying, in effect, "I want to die, but I really don't—I just want this pain to go away." The suicidal person may wish only a part of himself or herself to die, or to kill a "demon" inside. One expert actually suggests that intervention and treatment in a suicide attempt is much like a secular exorcism.

The Medical Dimension

The psychiatric community also points out that there is a medical dimension to suicide. Recent brain research suggests that depression can be organically based. For some, depression and other disturbances can be traced to the absence of certain elements in the brain's chemistry. That is why some who are being treated for depression take lithium in exact quantities—to restore the balance of this critical chemical in the brain. Others suffer from thyroid dysfunction. Still others suffer from hidden allergies which profoundly influence their mental balance and health.

No statistics are available to tell us how many suicides might be linked to physical causes; research continues in this field.

This makes it all the more important for helpers to refer those with suicidal tendencies to medical and psychiatric professionals. These specialists can often determine whether there is a medical problem, and, if so, develop a treatment plan.

For those whose disturbances are physically caused, suicide is a sickness—a symptom of mental illness more than a sinful moral decision. The person who commits suicide in the midst of an organically-based depression is morally responsible for his or her self-destruction, but the mental illness is a mitigating factor.

What about the influence of drugs and alcohol in suicidal thinking? One may be unable to make a rational, free choice while in the bondage of addiction. And many die a slow death due to addiction, whether they want to or not. Is this form of suicide based on a reasonable choice?

All these factors must lead us to question the assumption that the suicide choice is a rational one with which we should not interfere.

A Christian Response

Where does this leave us? What answer can our culture give to the question, "Why not suicide?" The "quality of life" must be questioned as a moral measure, for prevailing norms—narcissism, affluence, and insistence on instant solutions—challenge that quality at every turn. Many people cannot accept the sanctity of life, either, for they regard so little as sacred.

The Christian speaks prophetically in these circumstances, reaffirming that suicide is morally wrong in all situations. The church's teaching has not changed fundamentally in 2,000 years, though there is tremendous societal pressure to do so.

Our teaching has not changed, but our pastoral methods have. No longer do we—or should we—refuse a Christian burial for one who has committed suicide. The apostle Paul said that all have sinned and fall short of the glory of God (Rom. 3:23), and so it is with this kind of sinner. It is God's work to determine who may enter His presence.

As a pastor, then, I will err on the side of ministering in these circumstances. I try to explain that no one understands the immense complexity of suicide or the suicidal person. I try to help survivors know that God is with them in their hour of need. One way psychology has influenced me is to give me further insight into the brokenness of human beings, and the wonder of

God's redemption of that suffering.

In counseling the suicidal person, we can play an effective role. But we must understand that making propositional assertions with a suicidal person will not convince him or her of God's love, care, or even His presence. Rather, we need to win the person by prayer, love, and the presentation of hope.

Within the Christian community, however, we must categorically reassert the sanctity of human life which rejects suicide as an alternative. We need to be more like Job, who, in the midst of his suffering, remembered that he was God's creation:

Your hands shaped me and made me. Will you now turn and destroy me? Remember that you molded me like clay. Will you now turn me to dust again? Did you not pour me out like milk and curdle me like cheese, clothe me with skin and flesh and knit me together with bones and sinews? You gave me life and showed me kindness, and in your providence watched over my spirit. (Job 10:8-12)

If ever there were a person who should have committed suicide, it was Job! Yet Job understood that his life was a gift from God. Job was not to return the gift destroyed.

God's Word also affirms that creation was fashioned in God's will. When God created the human being, He did it in His image and breathed life into him, whereby the human became a living being (Gen. 1:27; 2:7). Life is a gift from God.

The third chapter of Genesis describes the Fall and the spiritual woes which followed. In the Book of Romans Paul teaches that we, as descendants of Adam, share in Adam's sin and despair. But there is righteousness, justification, salvation, hope, and life itself through Jesus Christ in His death and resurrection (Rom. 5:12-19).

The death and resurrection of Jesus Christ are the hope of the world. Christ is the incarnation of God and His will for human beings, that we might be in His fellowship and presence. God has never abandoned us, and never will. We can see this in the history of the people of Israel, for which Jesus is the culmination of all hopes and desires and covenants.

The suicidal person needs to know that God never abandons us to the power of death. God is with us even in our darkest hours, always faithful.

We see this in the Book of Lamentations, written during a terrible time when Jerusalem, that city where God said He would always dwell, was being overthrown. The people, thrown into utter despair, concluded that God was punishing and abandoning them. Yet even then, relying on God's faithfulness, they could find hope:

I have been deprived of peace; I have forgotten what prosperity is. So I say, "My splendor is gone and all that I had hoped from the Lord." I remember my affliction and my wandering, the bitterness and the gall. I well remember them, and my soul is downcast within me. Yet this I call to mind and therefore I have hope: Because of the Lord's great love we are not consumed, for his compassions never fail. (Lam. 3:17-22)

This historical testimony is very important, for its truth is objective. It does not depend on my subjective assent, my experience. Indeed, I need to evaluate my experiences and feelings against the objective truths of Scripture to see whether I am "on the beam."

If I feel abandoned by God, I need to square this feeling against the events and the nature of God revealed in Scripture. Then I see that my feeling is false, though I do not deny that I have felt that way. I am then faced with a choice: to believe something false because I rely on my experience, or to reevaluate my feelings and open up to what God may be teaching me. Will I submit myself to His authority, or declare myself and my experience to be the authority?

This is the choice faced by the suicidal person who confronts God's Word. Will he or she continue to feel abandoned by God if Scripture's overwhelming evidence is that God does not abandon His people? Is he or she so important that God makes an exception and abandons only him or her? All too often, the self-centeredness of suicidal thinking—and the thinking of our age—leads the person to answer, "Yes."

Hope: An Antidote

Why is this important? Because human life now is meant to be lived in hope. What is the ground of that hope? Jesus and His resurrection—His actual, physical resurrection from the dead, from the actual, empty tomb, as the New Testament writers are at such pains to note. If this is not the case, then, to borrow from

Paul, we are of all people most to be pitied. But Christ was raised, and has dealt a knockout blow to the power of sin and death in our lives. By the power of the Holy Spirit, the truth of Jesus' resurrection in history becomes the truth of His resurrection in our lives.

God's remembering and Jesus' resurrection—that is, a God who is faithful in history and in our histories—is the basis for our hope. He is our covenant Companion today, present in every dimension of our lives. Faced with this, the suicidal person must either (1) take the risk that God is there for him or her and admit that his or her own view is limited, or (2) take the risk that God is not there, contradicting a timeless view, and possibly be found wrong.

Again, however, we cannot state our hope as propositional truth and expect that the suicidal person will say, "Of course, you are absolutely right and I am wrong. I accept." Were that to happen, we would have to be deeply suspicious of the ease with which the truth was accepted. Instead, the helper becomes the incarnation of the truth of God's steadfast love, His constant remembrance.

The truth we proclaim must seep into the cracks of the suicidal person's soul. Our work is to help the person learn to live hopefully in a world that will not support that drive.

Those in a pastoral role can help by setting the tone in a local Body, proclaiming the hope and power of God in His Word and history. Thus strengthened, a congregation can become a beacon of hope in this world of darkness and despair. It all begins with the right handling of the Word as the medium of hope and as a call from God to the community and its members to trust.

Let me give you an example. Not too long ago I found myself slipping again into the abyss. I remember praying, "Lord, I think I've been here before. I claim your promise of steadfastness and love. But I also confess what I am feeling. Deliver me, O God." I was attending church, and prayed this as worship began.

During the service, one of the Scripture passages was Matthew 8:23-27, in which Jesus walks on water and calms the storm—and His disciples' fears. The preacher, in his sermon, showed that Jesus beckons us to take risks just as He invited Peter to walk on the water with Him. We need not fear, the preacher continued, for Jesus is always ready to receive us as we step out in faith. He illustrated the point with a story about a woman he had known who had grappled with depression. When the woman took the risk of believing in and claiming God's mercy and love for her, she began to find healing—though it did not come easily.

I was nearly in tears through the sermon. I saw that God could be present to me in my depression if I took the risk of believing that He would be there to receive me in Christ Jesus. Not that I would recover instantly, but I would be assured, or reassured, of God's continuing love for me. Later I talked with that pastor about my feelings, and began to get some insight on what really was at issue. I also learned to use some new tools to cope.

That pastor represented the Christian hope to me as he preached the Gospel. But he did not represent only himself, or the Lord Jesus Christ alone. He stood for the community of faith in which he labored, counseled, and preached. Our parishes and congregations must also be communities of hope and perseverance.

A Hopeful Community

A pastor, then, might be the most visible representative of God's hope and healing in Christ Jesus. But it really is the Christian community that can minister. We are members together, and have influence on one another. We are meant to be intimately related. As Paul says, "If one part suffers, every part suffers with it; if one part is honored, every part rejoices with it" (I Cor. 12:26).

The pastor is not the only one who hopes, and the pastor-counselee relationship is not a closed circle. The community is meant to minister, to make its hope real among its members, and to be a sign of hope in a broken world. Each of us in our congregations is a sign of Jesus' resurrection.

We need to be bold and clear about the hope that possesses us, to take the lead in a culture hoping against hope. As a community, and as individual members of a community, we must hurt with those who hurt, and dare to do so in hope.

Henri Nouwen puts it well in *The Wounded Healer: Ministry in Contemporary Society* (Doubleday, 1979): "A man can keep his sanity and stay alive as long as there is at least one person waiting for him." He observes, "Thousands of people commit suicide because there is nobody waiting for them tomorrow. There is no reason to live if there is nobody to live for." Every one of us can make a profound difference in the hurting person's life. "But when a man says to a fellow man, 'I will not let you go. I am going to be here tomorrow waiting for you and I expect you not to disappoint me,' then tomorrow is no longer an endless dark tunnel. It becomes flesh and blood in the brother who is waiting and for whom he wants to give life one more chance." This can be the vocation of every Christian.

But it does take some daring, and outreach to the despairing must be supported by the local Christian community. I was reminded of this when I proposed an advertisement for my denomination which would communicate that our congregations offer caring and compassion. A row of pictures would show hopeless situations, people in despair, with the caption, "Who Cares?" Below that would be a portrait of Christ with the caption, "He Cares." Under that would be pictures of church members with the caption, "We Care." At the bottom would appear the phrase, "The Caring Community," along with my denomination's name.

The ad was rejected by a denominational official, who shook his head sadly and said, "This isn't true." Upon reflection I had to admit that he was probably right—and that his evaluation did not apply only to my denomination.

If we are to have any impact on people who are considering suicide, we will have to reclaim the prophetic ministry of hope, grounded in Jesus Christ, our Redeemer. We will have to become active agents of hope in the unique places that God places us and opens before us.

This assertion goes beyond the pastoral care model which has dominated much of Christian training for the last 30 or 40 years, and which still has wide acceptance. That is a passive, accepting, and listening model. No doubt we must listen in loving compassion. But we must do more.

We need to assist the suicidal, not propositionally, but incarnationally. Let us not merely tell the person that there is a cup of cold water, of Living Water; let us bring the cup to her or him. Let us walk with the person through the valley of the shadow of death— with the map that, by God's grace and mercy, shows the way out.

The road to healing and recovery is long for the suicidal, so we must be patient, persevering, and persistent. We also must cooperate with and serve as allies of the professionals who treat them. And, as with so many kinds of recovery, we must walk with the suicidal a step at a time.

As our largely hopeless culture slides into further decay, we will have to be firm in our convictions that God has acted, God is acting, and God will continue to act in human history, in our own personal histories. We will have to be realistic about this life, and not become smug in our hope, because this hope does not emerge from our own power or insight. Rather we will desire urgently to share this hope with others in need.

CHAPTER SEVEN

LEGAL ISSUES

L ET US BE CLEAR FROM THE OUTSET: FOR YOUR PROTECTION in counseling and pastoring, you must know the specific laws of your state on the subject of suicide. States take varied approaches; this book can only provide a general overview of legal issues. For legal advice, please consult an attorney.

Suicide and the Law

Most states have decriminalized suicide. That is, only a few have laws defining the act of suicide itself as criminal or felonious. Many states used to outlaw suicide, but this practice was reversed for three reasons. First, laws did not deter the behavior. Second, courts and juries were reluctant to call a death suicide and impose legal penalties on the person's estate and survivors, thereby incurring public wrath for carrying out the law. Finally, there was increasing evidence that suicide is not a freely chosen act, but is much more often the result of mental illness.

Legal attention has shifted from the suicidal to those who have reason to believe suicide will be attempted. In many states, those with such knowledge are mandated to commit a person who is known to be mentally ill and a threat to society or self. While in the past few years there has been a shift away from committing the mentally ill, it is still true that, where danger exists to self or others, commitment is mandatory in these states.

What happens when a person is committed by a police officer or mental health professional? All 50 states allow a person who is in clear danger of harming himself or herself to be confined indefinitely until hospital personnel have determined that the person will not carry through with the suicide. The amount of time varies, but 48 hours is usually the minimum. With this commitment, the person's civil rights are removed; he or she cannot check himself or herself out. The length of stay and next referral are up to the psychiatric staff.

Why would the law mandate intervention? The background is found in English common law as expounded by Blackstone in the 19th century. According to this view, suicide is an affront against God, and against the king or queen, who has a duty to protect the well-being of all subjects. In American law, churches are given the responsibility to determine what might be an affront to God (sin). But the state still has the authority and responsibility to protect the general values of society, and the power of *parens patriae* (paternal authority) to protect individuals—even from themselves.

Our laws still generally reflect the belief that an individual's suicide is not without impact on anyone else. Suicide devalues life as a whole. There is also the "cluster effect" mentioned earlier in this book. When a suicide is committed, others may follow suit. The previous chapter described how this viewpoint has been challenged by libertarians who assert that the purpose of the state and its laws is to respect the inherent right of people to do as they please without government interference—so long as others do not suffer direct harm. This view is increasing in popularity in our culture.

Predictably, the legal issues of suicide revolve around money— namely, insurance payouts of death benefits. Insurance policies generally hold that benefits will not be paid to survivors if suicide was the cause of death. Insurers cover losses from accidents, not from choice. Most suicide-related legal battles today revolve around proof of suicide or accident for insurance purposes, not for criminal action.

William Masello, a county coroner in Virginia, writing in "The Proof of Law in Suicide" (*Journal of Forensic Science*, July 1986) notes that American courts have had a strong tendency to rule against suicide in a death. Suicide violates natural law, for one thing—the natural instinct of human beings to live and to preserve life. Then there must be clear and convincing proof of suicidal intent, resolution, and design. In the absence of a suicide note that design can be inferred, but is very difficult to prove. The courts have also been troubled in most jurisdictions by the lack of statutory laws clearly defining suicide, which provides no specific criteria for its certification. Many insurance companies have battled with survivors in court, and court rulings have not been consistent.

Suicide is no longer a criminal act in most states, but aiding and abetting suicide is. The vast majority of states have laws against assisting a suicide. One who assists a suicide is usually charged with murder or manslaughter; it is assumed that, while the suicidal person may be temporarily insane and therefore not criminally responsible for taking his or her own life, the same cannot be said for one who assists.

This may change as the euthanasia movement gains ground. Voters in California have been asked to consider allowing euthanasia under carefully monitored circumstances. Some advocates of the elderly want the aged to have the right to decide to terminate their lives when those lives are no longer "worth living." There was also the case of a paraplegic woman who did not want to continue living in her condition, but was physically unable to take her own life. She wanted the courts to require her doctors to withhold all treatment from her—even food and water. She did not want nourishment or medication forced on her, since she could not resist them herself. Her case attracted the attention of many who debated whether a person mentally alert and in command of her faculties, but physically unable to end her life, could order others to do that for her.

How cases like these are decided, and whether laws permitting "mercy-killing" are enacted, will have a bearing on whether those who aid suicide can be prosecuted. It will also affect laws that require intervention, potentially rendering intervention optional.

The Grace Community Case

At this writing, intervention is mandated for anyone who knows of an individual threatening suicide. If you fail to intervene, the state may or may not prosecute you. But the survivors of the person who committed suicide could also sue you for criminal negligence.

This is precisely what happened in a now-famous case involving the parents of 24-year-old Ken Nally and the staff and congregation of Grace Community Church in Sun Valley, California. The case, at this writing, is still open. It was dismissed by the original trial court after hearings; the parents appealed to a California state appeals court, which overturned the trial court's dismissal and remanded the case to that court for a retrial. Depending on the outcome of the case, it may eventually be brought for possible appeal to the California Supreme

Court, or a federal court. We will explore this case in some detail, for it raises many legal issues with which helpers must contend. For an excellent summary of the issues, see the February 1988 issue of *Church Law & Tax Report* and the article, "Clergy Malpractice—The Nally Case." Much of what follows is paraphrased from that report.

Ken Nally committed suicide during a period in which he was being counseled by lay pastors at Grace Church. Afterward, the parents sued the senior pastor, the counseling center, and the congregation for $1 million for negligence in the care of their son.

The argument for the plaintiffs took two directions. First, it was alleged that the church was negligent in not referring Nally to a licensed professional who could have dealt with his problems psychotherapeutically. Grace Church's counselors were not able to provide this service. On at least one occasion, however, the counselors did seek to refer Nally to professional help. Despite the advice of the counselors, Nally attempted suicide in March of 1979.

While hospitalized after this attempt, Nally talked with the church's senior pastor, John McArthur, in the presence of one of the counselors. Nally said he was sorry that the attempt had failed, and that when he was released he would attempt suicide again. These statements allegedly were never shared with Nally's parents or with the hospital physicians. One of the counselors said that doing so would have been like being at the scene of a fire, seeing the firefighters there, and calling the fire department.

After Nally's release, he stayed at the senior pastor's house for a few days. During that time the pastor encouraged Nally to see the physicians who had treated him. The young man never did, and in April 1979 he committed suicide.

The plaintiffs argued that the church had failed to prevent suicide and were liable for this neglect and event. When this case was remanded to the original trial court for reconsideration, the church's counsel said the fact remained that, in the weeks before Nally's suicide, he was seen by five physicians and a psychiatrist. The court ruled 2-1, however, that the church was indeed liable for the act, since it was acting in a counseling relationship with the young man.

The two majority judges allowed that "it is clear that a

bystander watching someone about to jump off a cliff has no duty to attempt to prevent that suicide, nor would he have a duty to suggest the individual see a psychologist or enter a psychiatric hospital." There is no legal requirement to be a good Samaritan. Nor is there a duty to refer a suicidal person to professional help, the judges said, if you are a friend who is consulted by a emotionally disturbed acquaintance seeking personal counsel; a worker on a counseling hotline or other form of short-term counseling service; or a pastor who has a casual conversation with an emotionally disturbed person at, say, the back of the church. In none of these circumstances is a "counseling relationship" established, the judges said, so there is no "duty to refer."

But the judges also held that if you approach a person to offer counsel on emotional problems that are leading him or her to commit suicide, California law imposes a duty to take preventive measures if a suicide appears likely. This is true for both licensed professionals and counselors "who hold themselves out as capable of dealing with mental and emotional illness severe enough to lead to suicide." There is also a clear duty to refer in such cases.

Since the court said that "non-therapist" counselors have less education and experience in treating severe emotional disorders, "they have no duty to take appropriate precautions against a suicide unless that suicide is foreseeable to them." In this case, the court felt the potential should have been obvious; Nally had attempted to take his life and was clear in his intention to attempt it again.

Once a suicide is foreseeable to a non-therapist counselor, his or her primary duty is to refer to a specialist who can engage in primary treatment and prescribe medication if that is necessary. If the counselee resists this suggestion, the counselor has a duty to inform those who are in a position to take clear and specific action.

Furthermore, the judges said, counselors are not the only ones with a duty to refer. The church sponsoring a counseling program must be certain that its counselors are aware of these responsibilities.

The court concluded that Nally's suicide was foreseeable and preventable, and that the church counselors knew this and failed to refer. Therefore, they "failed to satisfy the non-therapist counselor's minimal standard of care by neglecting to refer Nally to psychiatrists or a psychiatric hospital or other mental health professionals . . . authorized and equipped to minimize the risk Nally would commit suicide." In the same vein, the church failed "to train its counselors in their responsibilities to refer suicidal counselees or to otherwise insure that they were aware of those responsibilities." Thus the charge of negligence was made, for which the church stood liable.

The other charge was of "reckless and outrageous conduct" and "intentional infliction of emotional distress" that contributed to Nally's death. The key piece of evidence was a tape in which one of the Grace Church counselors described his beliefs about the status of a believer who commits suicide. This tape was made in 1981, two years after Nally's death.

The trial court did not allow the tape to be introduced as evidence, but the appeals court instructed the trial court in its rehearing to admit the tape as evidence. The appeals court stated that nothing in the ruling should predetermine the defendants' liability for reckless conduct, but that there was admissible evidence to support the plaintiff's claim of liability and injury. Even though the tape was made two years after the event, the statements on it were "relevant to prove the probable content of the counseling the defendants offered the plaintiffs' suicidal son."

The tape in question was titled, "Principles of Biblical Counseling," and was used in training new counselors. It included the following comment:

And the suicidal says, "I am under such tremendous pressure, now I've got to have the pleasure of release! Now! I don't care about the future." That's characteristic of human nature. So it is very characteristic of the suicidal that it is his fear of judgment that drives him into the death after which he will face that judgment, if he's an unbeliever. And after which if he is a believer, he'll go to be with the Lord. Yes, there'll be a loss of reward, but because of the Lord and His grace he'll go to be with the Lord. In fact, suicide is one of the ways that the Lord takes home a disobedient believer. We read that in the Bible. That death is one of the ways that the Lord deals with us. In I Corinthians 11:30 it [says], "For this reason because you are not judging sin in your own life, many among you are weak and sick," and what? "a number sleep!" What's that mean? They're dead! That's right. And suicide for a believer is the Lord saying, "Okay, come on home. Can't use you anymore on earth. If you're not going to deal with those things in your life, come on home."

On the strength of this evidence, the plaintiffs could charge reckless and outrageous conduct. It appeared that the counseling did not deter suicide, but perhaps encouraged the practice.

But can't a church teach what it sincerely and profoundly believes, even in counseling, without interference by the state with its First Amendment rights? Would religious freedom be damaged as the government mandated what a faith group ought to teach, or how it ought to counsel?

The court said no on two counts. First, none of the church's staff had testified that it would have been a violation of his or her beliefs, doctrines, or counseling practices to refer a person to secular psychiatric professionals. So the counselors did not hold a religious belief that would have to be abandoned to comply with the duty to refer.

Second, the judges held that there are times when the compelling interests of the state must override religious freedom. The prevention of a suicide is one of those compelling interests. The dissenting judge argued that this would constitute a burden on the free exercise of religion, and that the state's reason for intervention must be "essential" to the accomplishment of legislated policy.

The majority judges said that any burden on religious beliefs imposed by the duty to refer was too minimal to constitute a denial of the guaranty of religious freedom. Indeed, the church may counsel whomever it chooses. It may base its principles on religious doctrine. And it may use any reference from Scripture that it chooses. The only limitation is that if the church knows of someone who is suicidal, it must refer that person to therapeutic help.

The court claimed that it was not discriminating against religion in this case, only requiring church counselors to abide by the same duty to refer as would be required of any "non-therapist" counselors. If it did not require this of church counselors, the court said, then the decision would favor, rather than discriminate against, the exercise of religion by making an exception for churches.

The issue of confidentiality between parishioner and pastor was also raised. If a suicidal person resists the counselor's advice to seek professional help and will not accept the referral, the counselor is obliged to contact loved ones or a psychological professional. Would this be a breach of the confidential relationship in counseling? No, said the judges. When the counselee's life is at stake, the interest in disclosure overtakes the duty to maintain confidential information. This applies even to the pastor of a church, since the traditional bond of cleric and penitent in a confessing relationship "does not apply to communications between a pastoral counselor and his counselee."

The court made it clear, however, that this case did not deal with "clergy malpractice." The majority opinion stated, "This case has little or nothing to say about the liability of clergymen for the negligent performance of their ordinary ministerial duties or even their counseling duties except when they enter into a counseling relationship with suicidal individuals."

This case refers *only* to California law, and is only an interim opinion, since at this writing the case has been remanded to the original trial court and Grace Community Church has appealed this decision. But it teaches many important lessons for those who counsel in churches. The case is being watched closely, as it is breaking new ground in the legal responsibilities that church counseling centers have in dealing with the despondent and the suicidal.

Could You Be Sued?

Churches are not the only targets of litigation. In Tennessee, officials and counselors at the Montgomery County Girls Home, the Cumberland Valley Girls Home, the Harriet Cohn Mental Health Center, Middle Tennessee Children and Youth Services, and the owner of the Lebanon (Tennessee) Group Home have been defendants in an $8 million suit brought by Melody Murphy, mother of Tara Toten. Tara committed suicide in December 1984 in the Lebanon Group Home after she had been told that she would not be allowed to go home for Christmas.

The suit alleged that Tara's death was caused by negligence of the state, the homes, and the centers. The defense attorney opened the case, however, by saying that there was no indication that Tara was suicidal. "She was not withdrawn or depressed," the attorney said. "She did not write letters to anyone saying that she was contemplating suicide. She was quite the opposite."

Many more cases are being brought to trial citing negligence, incompetence of a counselor, and intentional infliction of emotional distress. We should expect to see even more legal action in this area.

What does this mean to you and your church? First, you need to keep in mind basic legal principles regarding suicide. Here's a review:

1. In nearly every state, suicide has been decriminalized. The action, by itself, carries no penalty to the estate or the survivor in these states. In insurance claims, however, proof of suicide is a clear reason for denying payment of benefits.

2. In the vast majority of states, assisting a suicide is a crime. Unless "mercy-killing" laws are widely adopted and loosely interpreted, this sanction will most likely remain.

3. One is not legally liable for a suicidal death unless one has entered into a counseling relationship with that individual (though there may be, for the Christian, a moral liability). In many states (particularly in California), if one has entered into a counseling relationship with a person who is likely to commit suicide, the counselor has a duty to refer the person to a mental health professional who is competent to handle him or her.

If a church develops a counseling ministry, therefore, and that counseling involves working with severely depressed or despairing people, that congregation must be absolutely clear about its legal responsibilities in the state where it operates. That church must carefully prepare a list of referring agencies and individuals, or have licensed and degreed professionals on staff. This would be true if the church offered person-to-person or person-to-group counseling, or even if it had a telephone hotline (though at this writing, in California, that hotline would not be covered by the appeals court ruling). If you do not know the law, you are setting yourself and your congregation up for some potentially expensive nightmares.

Only you and your congregation can assess whether reaching out to suicidal people is worth the legal risk. The Nally case has, for the time being, heightened the risk for non-therapist counselors. The counselor who does not refer someone he or she knows to be suicidal (and who does commit suicide) is open to legal liability. If the counselee resists the referral, the counselor has a duty to inform those in a position to prevent the counselee's suicide. Counselors who do not understand these points are no less negligent, and the church is much more negligent. This is true only in California for now, but other states with similar cases will be looking for guidance from the Nally case.

Churches with counseling ministries should adopt a policy statement in accord with the Nally principles, even if they do not operate in California. That policy statement must be communicated to all church counselors.

Churches with counseling ministries should also review their general liability insurance policies. Many denominations have such policies through their own insurance programs, or have access to such coverage.

If your liability insurance covers counseling and would cover an alleged incident, the policy should provide for legal defense and compensation up to the limits of the policy. If you were sued beyond the limits of your policy, you would be wise to secure independent counsel to defend your church and counselors against damages that exceed your policy limits. It is possible that, with such liability insurance, your church would become a more attractive target for lawsuits—but you would want to weigh that against being sued without any coverage at all.

The Counselor-Counselee Relationship

How should you treat the issue of confidentiality? Let us return to the point the California court made about the difference between a cleric-penitent relationship, which is honored by "the seal of the confessional," and the counselor-counselee relationship. The privilege granted to the cleric could not be granted to the counselor in the case of suicide.

As Richard R. Hammer, editor of *Church Law and Tax Report* observes, "While the court concluded that the interest in disclosing confidential information about a counselee's suicidal tendencies outweighs any policy favoring the confidentiality of counselor-counselee communications, this conclusion certainly is not self-evident and may be rejected by courts in other jurisdictions." Cast into doubt also is the cleric-penitent privilege: "The court's conclusion that the clergyman-penitent privilege does not apply in the context of pastoral counseling is a bizarre ruling that has little if any basis in law."

So the law is unclear at present regarding pastoral counseling in suicidal situations. This does not mean that churches and individuals should shy away from such counseling. It does mean that great care should be taken to see that potential counselors understand their responsibilities. We may well need to err on the side of disclosure and active intervention if, insofar as we are able to determine, a suicide is imminent.

Shifting the Blame?

The situation is even less clear with teens and children who are suicidal. Take the case of a 13-year-old boy in Connecticut who killed himself at home after school. The boy's father sued public school officials for not knowing that his son was upset and suicidal, and for negligence thereby in not intervening. As the father's lawyer told *The New York Times*, the suit was intended "to change the way schools do business."

How? Perhaps schools would have to be responsible for children's activities on and off the school grounds, and for knowing children well enough to detect emotional problems. But as Gary Marx of the American Association of School Administrators says, "It is unreasonable that a parent would try to hold the school responsible for being the sole detector of the condition that you would expect parents to identify in the first place." He continues, "The school often is the institution we have looked to to help solve many of the problems of society, but the school has some limitations. The school can't always be the substitute for the parent. Parents and others in society also must accept their responsibilities for what happens to children."

When the blame for suicide is shifted onto institutions such as the school and church, the result is that counseling is increasingly risky. It is also more risky to set up a formal pastoral counseling ministry, or even an informal lay counseling team. Who would want to volunteer with the possibility of being sued? If the counseling ministry is even quasi-independent, who would want to serve on a board and risk being sued individually as well as corporately? These questions will have to be addressed by any congregation wanting to set up any kind of program—and be reviewed carefully by congregations with such programs in place.

Psychologists, psychiatrists, hospitals, social workers, nurses, physicians, guidance and vocational counselors, and even lawyers are being sued by survivors for alleged responsibility—even complicity—in the suicides of loved ones. Churches and schools are not the only groups in legal trouble.

Even elements of popular culture are not immune from liability. Earlier in this book the case of Raymond Belknap, an 18-year-old who committed suicide, was described. According to the lawsuit, Belknap and his friend James Vance, while smoking marijuana and drinking, listened to the album *Stained Class* by the British heavy metal rock band Judas Priest. The two young men then went to a nearby church playground. Belknap shot himself in the head, killing himself instantly. Vance twitched at the last moment, shooting part of his face away, but surviving.

The lawsuit, filed by Vance and by Belknap's mother, asserted that the lyrics to the music combined with the heavy metal sound mesmerized the youths, convincing them that "the answer to life was death." The suit asks for monetary damages. It names Judas Priest, CBS Records, and the record store in Sparks, Nevada that sold the album to Belknap.

While the survivors say the music and lyrics led to Belknap's death—suggesting he was not responsible for his choice—attorneys for Judas Priest and CBS planned to base their defense on the First Amendment constitutional right of freedom of expression. Similar cases have been thrown out of court on those grounds.

Elliott Hoffman, the band's attorney, stepped beyond the First Amendment argument to the content of the music. "There isn't anything in these lyrics that discusses life, death, mortality, violence, or anything else. Indeed, they are a pretty innocuous set of words, put together with the music because they rhyme." Hoffman concluded that an adult could easily put together a list of ten songs that suggest death, citing lyrics like, "I just can't live another day without you." But at this writing the Washoe County court appears ready to explore the case in some detail, lining up expert witnesses in psychology, psychiatry, hypnotism, theology, and bioacoustics, the study of how the body and mind react to sounds like music.

A State of Confusion

The legal confusion is interesting, for it returns to a question of values—particularly the value of responsibility. Who is responsible in a suicide?

If the libertarians had their way, the law would recognize that the free moral agent made a choice based on a rational decision about the good for his or her life. Psychiatrists and psychologists would say that suicide is a sign or form of mental illness, so that the person is at least partly absolved of responsibility. Insurance companies would say the person is responsible for the act. Some angry survivors would seek anyone or anything beyond themselves to legally nail with some measure of responsibility. To their way of thinking, there has to be someone to blame.

But is there? That is a much less resolved legal question than we might think. For now, there is the blame that can be placed on a counselor if a formal counseling relationship existed.

But how can even that be proved conclusively? And what constitutes a "non-therapist" counselor? How are we to recognize who has the ability to treat a suicidal person? And what happens if there is no one to refer to in smaller communities, or if time does not permit the referral?

These questions all remain unresolved. Just about anyone can hang out a shingle and call herself or himself a therapist or counselor. And there are a bewildering array of therapies with a variety of philosophical bases, all the way from humanistic psychology to behavior modification. There are Freudians, Rogerians, Adlerians, Skinnerians, Jungians and more.

What is the standard for evaluating professional credentials in a referral, or in a lawsuit involving that referral? Again, the question is unresolved. The California court did insist that the particular bases of counseling were not of concern, only the duty to refer. But that does not quite make sense if the difference between a "non-therapist" and a "therapist" counselor cannot be articulated. There will be many more lawsuits before these questions are finally resolved.

Where Are We Headed?

An even more complex legal web is being spun by the development of proposed laws legalizing euthanasia. Legislators will have to determine guidelines for allowing the taking of one's own life—while retaining the laws that uphold the duty to intervene in a suicide.

Lawmakers may try to distinguish between committing suicide in the prime of life and doing so when death is imminent. But who is to judge whether one is in the prime of life or in the midst of death? It all depends on the angle of vision. Many suicidal people believe that, functionally, they have died. Now all they want is to make objectively real what they feel subjectively to be true. Would you like to be the judge, or on the jury, trying to sort out such a case? Would you like to be the counselor who had to choose whether or not to intervene?

In a secular society we should expect many more legal entanglements between the prerogatives of the state and the free exercise of religion. The state, while increasingly emphasizing the quality of life over the sanctity of life, will also intervene more and more to protect what it sees as individual rights. The Church's stand on the sanctity of life and the legal confusion over responsibility could eventually lead to this scenario:

At a denominational hospital that receives government funds, a lawsuit is brought against the hospital, its board, administrators, and chaplains. The charge is "intentional infliction of emotional distress" on a family who decided with an elder loved one to opt for euthanasia. Family members were "interfered with" by the hospital chaplain who encouraged them to consider the sanctity of life. At the same time, the same hospital is sued by the parents of an adolescent who, upon discharge from the psychiatric unit of the hospital, committed suicide. The parents charge that the hospital should have been more aware of the possibility and intervened.

Is this scenario outlandish? Maybe not. Already limits are being set on the function of a full-time chaplain at a public hospital. A federal court in Iowa recently rejected the claim that the employment of a full-time chaplain violated the First Amendment's nonestablishment of religion clause. But, saying that the chaplain's work could not be unrestricted, the court ruled that he could not evangelize, and could not counsel employees or outpatients or families who were not in the hospital for emergencies or to visit dying loved ones. Nor could the chaplain have access to medical records without the express approval of the patient or guardian.

How much longer will these restrictions apply only to public hospitals? Other pastoral counseling services could eventually be regulated, too.

Church leaders must look ahead to anticipate how their work with suicidal persons will be affected by legal trends. At least one board member per church should be responsible for monitoring legal developments so that the church and its counseling can be in line with government regulation and oversight—or to challenge these should that be necessary. If a church board member will not do this, it may be necessary to form an advisory committee for pastoral counseling which can perform many of the functions of a separate board of trustees—without having to incorporate as a separate entity.

Despite the legal queasiness surrounding the issue of suicide and its treatment, churches should involve themselves in counseling the suicidal—as long as the churches understand the training required and the limitations placed on counselors. That may not be such a bad thing, for it promotes teamwork among helpers.

Legal questions will only get more complex in the next few years, while the suicide rate continues to climb. Yet in the midst of all this, God still calls us to work.

BIBLIOGRAPHY

The body of literature on suicide is increasing—but still is not as large as one might expect. And the amount that is specifically Christian is very small. If you want to read more about suicide, read secular sources carefully and critically, comparing their positions to ones you as a Christian take.

Books and Articles

Here are two books, written from a Christian point of view, which I recommend:

Bill Blackburn's *What You Should Know About Suicide* (Waco, Texas: Word, 1982) is a good, basic introduction to the subject from a Christian perspective.

Jerry Johnston's *Why Suicide? What Parents and Teachers Must Know to Save Our Kids* (Nashville: Thomas Nelson Publishers, 1987) is a compelling and readable confrontation of teen suicide. Johnston himself admits that his "is not the definitive work on this subject. It is not intended to be a textbook." It is strong on narrative and firsthand accounts from his ministry, and thin on legal matters and psychological theory. But it is the sort of book I would put in the hands of parents who worry about suicide among their own teens and in their communities.

From a Jewish point of view, Dr. Sol Gordon, Professor of Child and Family Studies at Syracuse University Institute for Family Research and Education, has written *When Living Hurts* (New York: Union of American Hebrew Congregations, 1985). Gordon writes from a humane and sensitive perspective. It is the sort of book you could give a teen.

Jane Lederer's *Dead Serious: A Book for Teenagers about Teenager Suicide* (New York: Atheneum, 1987) is directed to teens, especially those with no particular religious affiliation. Since teenagers can spot propaganda and moralizing a mile away, it is important to get into their hands literature that truly communicates with them. Evidently this book does; it is a hot

113

property in the young adult section of my town's public library.

A more thorough study of teens, written from a secular perspective for adults, is Jerry Jacobs' *Adolescent Suicide* (New York: Irvington Publishers, 1980). If it is true, as someone once told me, that a new generation gap develops every four years, you may find some of the material outdated. But it is still a good resource.

Little has been written that focuses on suicide among the elderly; most of the publishing attention in this area seems oriented more toward questions of euthanasia than to suicide. In this book we have noted Doris Portwood's *Commonsense Suicide: The Final Right* (Hemlock Society, 1983). It will make for unsettling reading if you clearly advocate the sanctity of life. But her argument—that the elderly have a right as free persons to make choices about their lives and deaths—needs to be understood, if for no other reason than that it is being voiced more and more often these days.

How shall we deal with the survivors of loved ones who have committed suicide? One of the few books available on the subject is Iris Bolton's *My Son, My Son: A Guide to Healing after Death, Loss, and Suicide* (Atlanta: Bolton Press, 1987). She explores grief over sudden loss and death, which, as any pastor or counselor knows, is a sharply painful path.

On more general themes of grief and bereavement, a Christian classic is C. S. Lewis' *A Grief Observed* (available in a variety of editions).

A secular classic on the subject is Colin Murray Parkes' *Bereavement: Studies of Grief in Adult Life* (New York: Pelican Books, 1975). Parkes is helpful in his exposition of seven elements common to bereavement and loss. When he wrote the book he was lecturer at London Hospital Medical College and a respected psychiatrist; this work is the fruit of several years of study and reflection on the subject, and is based on interviews with widows and widowers, as well as clinical information and observation.

A brief book written for ministers and lay counselors is Doug Manning's *Comforting Those Who Grieve: A Guide for Helping Others* (San Francisco: Harper and Row, 1985). This is a warm book by a Baptist minister who has a winsome way of getting at a difficult subject. This book would be a good training manual for those in a congregation who want to develop a grief ministry—particularly to those who have lost a loved one to suicide.

A general book to help the suicidal, their loved ones, and those who minister to both is Paul G. Quinnett's *Suicide: The Forever Decision* (New York: Continuum, 1987). Dr. Quinnett is the Director of Adult Services at Spokane (Washington) Community Mental Health Center, and a clinical psychologist and practicing therapist. His is a warm and approachable book. It is not technical nor theoretical. But it also is not a clearly Christian book. Most Christians will not object to the book, but may wish to complement the reading with biblical and theological reflection.

An older book, but still a very good source for basic information on suicide, is Edward Robb Ellis' *The Traitor Within: Our Suicide Problem* (Garden City, New York: Doubleday and Sons, 1961).

In *Suicide: The Hidden Epidemic* (New York: Watts, 1986), Margaret Hyde explores the world of the "accidental death" as well as more clearly suicidal deaths to provide a more complete picture of suicide in the U.S.

Another good general survey for the inquisitive layperson is Jacques Choron's *Suicide* (New York: Charles Scribners' Sons, 1972).

An excellent interdisciplinary study of suicide is *The Savage God: A Study of Suicide* by A. Alvarez (New York: Random House, 1972). Alvarez is, first and foremost, a literary critic, so he devotes a good portion of his work to examining the phenomenon of suicide in literature. This part of the book is fascinating. He also deals with the psychological and intellectual sides of suicide, casting a critical eye on various psychological explanations—one of the few places such a treatment can be found. From an aesthetic point of view, the book is exceptionally well-written. Alas, at this time it is out of print.

Psychological studies on suicide are not as plentiful as might be expected. Perhaps A. Alvarez was right in his observation that suicide has not been studied often by psychiatrists and psychoanalysts because suicide can indicate that their therapies have failed. In any case, here are what I think to be the best sources:

First, there is Emile Durkheim's classic sociological study of suicide to which we have referred in this book, *Suicide: A Study in Sociology* (New York: The Free Press, 1966). Durkheim pioneered the study of the phenomenon as he tried to get at social causes for an essentially individual act.

Maurice L. Farber's *Theory of Suicide* (New York: Arno Press, 1977), as we have noted, balances the individual and social aspects of suicidal behavior.

Irving Berent's *The Algebra of Suicide* (New York: Human Science Press, 1981) gets at the twisted logic employed by the suicidal person to justify his or her act.

But the best discussion of all in this area is Edwin S. Shneidman's *Definition of Suicide* (New York: John Wiley, 1985), a basic primer for the entire field. It does get a little clinical from time to time, but is certainly not impenetrable for the thoughtful student. A good introduction to Shneidman's thinking is contained in his article for *Psychology Today,* "At the Point of No Return" (March 1987).

One book deals with the theory that the act of suicide is not solely individual, but may occur in clusters. It is *Suicide Clusters* by Loren Coleman (Boston: Faber and Faber, 1987). It is based on recent research into this phenomenon.

I could locate only one book dealing specifically with prevention: Louis Wekstein's *A Handbook of Suicidology: Principles, Problems, and Practices* (New York: Brunner/Mazel, 1979). Even Wekstein deals with prevention only in the context of other areas, however. This book can be heavy reading, and is not intended for the typical church parishioner.

At this writing nothing seems available in book form on the legal issues involved in suicide. But there are a few outstanding law review articles. One in particular is a gold mine of information: "Suicide: A Constitutional Right?" by Thomas J. Marzen, et al in the *Duquesne Law Review* (Fall 1985).

In this book the following were also cited: "Suicide and Assisting Suicide: A Critique of Legal Sanctions" by Michele Malloy and H. Tristram Englehardt, Jr. in the *Southwestern Law Journal* (November 1982); "The Proof of Law of Suicide" by William Massello in the *Journal of Forensic Science* (July 1986); and "The Role of Law in Suicide Prevention: Beyond Civil Commitment—a Bystander Duty to Report Suicide Threats" by Kate E. Bloch in the *Stanford Law Review* (April 1987).

The pastor and the church board will want to review *Clergy Malpractice* by H. Newton Malony, et al (Philadelphia: Westminster,

1987). The authors examine many varieties of legal action that may be taken against ministers and churches when a mistake is made—and even when one isn't.

Organizations

In addition to published resources, some organizations can be of help to those who wish to serve the suicidal and their loved ones.

The American Association of Suicidology provides data on suicide and information on support groups, but not specific psychiatric referral nor telephone hotline counseling. To contact the association, write Ms. Julie Perlman, M.S.W., Executive Office, American Association of Suicidology, 2459 South Ash Street, Denver, CO 80222. Or call (303) 692-0985.

For information on community mental health clinics, call the National Mental Health Association at (703) 684-7722. This organization is also a good source for general information on suicide and its prevention. Its mailing address is 1021 Prince Street, Alexandria, VA 22314.

To locate a therapist who specializes in working with suicidal teens, contact the American Psychiatric Association at (202) 682-6000; the American Psychological Association at (202) 955-7600; or the National Association of Social Workers at (202) 565-0333.

You could also check with the Salvation Army in your area. In many places this organization runs a counseling service which may involve suicide prevention.

Another helpful organization is The Samaritans. Check your local phone directory to find out whether there is a chapter in your area. The Samaritans assist suicidal people in finding help. The group operates hotlines in many areas. You may want to offer your help as a hotline counselor; training sessions for volunteers may be provided by the group.

I have revised much of this book during Holy Week. In fact, I am putting these words down on the eve of Easter, that day when the Church cries out around the world, "Alleluia! Christ is risen indeed!"

Somehow it is all quite fitting. This cry is for life, which has not been vanquished or extinguished by the power of sin and death. God indeed has the last word.

Yet Easter does not come easily. Indeed, the struggle for life is often difficult and frightening. We must pass through the wickedness of Golgotha to hear Jesus' invitation to go on with Him to Galilee, to be where He said He would be. As the old Gospel hymn says, "If you can't bear the cross, then you can't wear the crown."

In the Episcopal Church, the psalm appointed to be read on Good Friday is Psalm 88. Have you ever heard an exposition from the pulpit of Psalm 88? Have you read it much? You should. It certainly gives haunting voice to the dark night of the soul—and it found its way into the Bible as God's very Word, too. This psalm does not end with a praise to God, but with a bitter comment after some imploring questions to the Lord that get at the very nub of the Christian faith:

> Do you show your wonders to the dead?
> Do those who are dead rise up and praise you?
> Is your love declared in the grave,
> your faithfulness in Destruction?
> Are your wonders known in the places of darkness,
> or your righteous deeds in the land of oblivion?
> But I cry to you for help, O Lord;
> in the morning my prayer comes before you.
> Why, O Lord, do you reject me and hide your face
> from me?   (Ps. 88:10-14)

The psalm ends in shocking despair: "You have taken my companions and loved ones from me; the darkness is my closest friend" (Ps. 88:18). You can almost see David burying his head in his hands or staring off vacantly into space—at nothing.

I was like that once, long before I knew of Psalm 88. The moment I first came across the psalm, however, I recognized myself in those words. I had by then accepted the objective truth of God's revealed Word. Now I knew that God's Word was true for me, too. The Bible was not some erudite, musty-but-sacred book to be revered and not read. It was God's Word in the guts and grit of life.

As I read the words, I pondered in prayer how I had felt long before when darkness had been my closest friend. I remembered hot summer nights in my stuffy, airless room on the top floor of an apartment house, my drapes drawn as I sat in darkness and silence. I had been thinking about nothing, but was overwhelmed with heaviness and an almost palpable, indescribable sadness which pervaded every bone and sinew. I probably actually ached with sadness. I just wanted to sleep—forever, peacefully, not fitfully. I wanted no dreams instead of the troubling ones from which I had been awakening, drenched with sweat, some of it from the stifling heat and some of it from the oppressiveness I felt within.

I wish I could say that on that sweltering night I came to know Jesus Christ as my personal Lord and Savior, and that everything was instantly all right—that I was cured and sitting up, clothed and in my right mind (to paraphrase the Gospel writers' description of one who had been healed by Jesus). No, Jesus did not come to me then. I was not healed. But I was saved, quite literally, from extinguishing myself. As I look back, I now know that it was the sovereign and loving grace of God at work even before I knew it.

I do not pretend to understand the mystery of the operation of this grace in my life. But I did not fall into that dreadful sleep I had planned on. I am very glad that I didn't. That sounds trite; I am grateful that I didn't, grateful to God, grateful to me.

To have committed suicide would have been a very stupid thing to do, and a very cowardly thing. Somehow I presumed in my weary, adolescent wisdom that I knew all there was to know of life, and now I had reached The End. I'm grateful to have stuck around to see what life holds. There is much to rejoice in, if the eyes of your heart are open to see.

That opening happened when Jesus Christ came into my life. When He did, I felt no magical turnaround. I did not sense that, as the hymn says, my life "would be all sunshine in the sweetness of the Lord." But there was an awakening in my life.

Awakening. What a word for those who have lived through the night hours of suicidal despair, and for those who work with such people. We helpers are like those who come into the darkened room and shake the person awake, saying, "Wake up! The day is here!"

That is the difference we with a Christian perspective and commitment can offer in working with the suicidal. It allows the suicidal to fill the spiritual void with the light of Christ. It is the fact that Jesus has faced the agony of death, that when He suffered death on the cross He bore every conceivable pain and guilt and sin that may weigh us down. He is raised from the dead, and in Him only do we truly find our resurrection from that which would propel us to die.

For a while, that hope may not be clear to us. We have to get used to the light.

It's a strange, wonderful, sometimes painful, sometimes joyful, always adventurous life. But I am alive! And those to whom you minister can be alive! And it all is because Christ is risen to life.

Because He lives, we live. Alleluia!